Mary O'Malley

LOOK OUT . . . HERE COMES TROUBLE!

AMBER LANE PRESS

All rights whatsoever in this play are strictly
reserved and application for performance, etc.,
should be made before rehearsal to:
Dr. Jan Van Loewen Ltd.,
81-83 Shaftesbury Avenue,
London W1V 8BX.

No performance may be given unless a licence
has been obtained.

First published in 1979 by
Amber Lane Productions Limited,
Amber Lane Farmhouse,
The Slack,
Ashover, Derbyshire S45 0EB.

Printed by A. Wheaton & Co. Ltd., Exeter

ISBN 0 906399 04 1

Look Out . . . Here Comes Trouble! was first produced at the Warehouse, Donmar Theatre, London on 16 November, 1978. It was directed by John Caird and designed by Sue Plummer, with the following cast:

DENNIS	Edwin Richfield
WALLY	Brian Hayes
VICKY	Deirdra Morris
TREVOR	Charles Wegner
JANET	Jane Carr
DR WILSON	Nicholas Le Prevost
SYLVIA	Gaye Brown
OLIVE	Maxine Audley
BRIAN	Peter Clough
KIERAN	John Rogan
MRS O'TOOLE	Doreen Keogh
CYRIL	Jeffery Kissoon
NIGHT NURSE	Denyse Alexander
GEORGE	Nigel Terry

AMBER LANE PLAYS

Series Editor: Judith Scott

Also available in this series:

Whose Life is it Anyway?   *by Brian Clark*

Once a Catholic   *by Mary O'Malley*

Funny Peculiar   *by Mike Stott*

For information on these and forthcoming titles write to:

Amber Lane Press,
Amber Lane Farmhouse
The Slack
Ashover
Derbyshire S45 0EB

Characters

DENNIS	A Londoner in his early forties. He wears suits and has a short-back-and-sides haircut.
WALLY	A Londoner in his fifties. He is over-weight and scruffy.
TREVOR	An incoherent alcoholic in his thirties. He plays the saxophone.
KIERAN	An Irishman in his fifties.
MRS O'TOOLE	Kieran's wife. A big Irish woman who wears trousers and has short hair.
JANET	A Londoner in her early thirties. Pretty and immature for her years.
SYLVIA	A Londoner in her late thirties. She has long hair, brightly hennaed, and wears tight trousers (sometimes satin) and very high heels.
OLIVE	A stout, middle-aged woman with unruly hair.
GEORGE	A Londoner in his late twenties. He has a beard, permed hair and tinted glasses.
BRIAN	Sylvia's boyfriend. A weedy Northerner in his early thirties.
DR WILSON	A psychiatrist in his thirties. He wears a brown corduroy jacket sprinkled with dandruff.
VICKY	The Ward Sister. About thirty. Tall, long-haired and elegantly dressed in the latest vogue.
CYRIL	A happy-go-lucky West Indian nurse. Smartly dressed in light suits and lots of gold jewellery.
NIGHT NURSE	A short, fat, middle-aged woman in nurse's uniform. Bossy, with a strong London accent.

The action takes place in a mental hospital in London.

ACT ONE

SCENE ONE

The lounge. The radio is playing a pop song from a commercial radio station. WALLY *is dozing on the couch. He is holding on to a bulging plastic carrier bag from a supermarket.* TREVOR *walks past angrily with a bottle of milk in his hand.* VICKY *comes in with* JANET *behind her carrying a suitcase. They go into the female dormitory.* KIERAN *comes out of the male dormitory in his vest and underpants. He runs off.* DENNIS *comes in with two cups of tea. He nudges* WALLY.

DENNIS: Cup of tea, Wally?

WALLY: Oh. Thanks very much.

DENNIS: You listening to that by any chance?

WALLY: Yeah.

DENNIS: Oh. Because if you wasn't, I was going to turn it off.

> [DENNIS *takes the carrier bag from* WALLY *and brings out 2 lbs of sugar. They both put sugar in their tea.*]

WALLY: You can turn it off if you like. I was only waiting to hear if they was going to play one by whatsername. You know . . .

DENNIS: Shirley Bassey.

WALLY: That's right. They don't seem to play her as much as they used to.

DENNIS: Perhaps you ought to write up and ask them.

WALLY: What, like a request, you mean?

DENNIS: Yeah. Why not?

WALLY: I wouldn't have to put the address, would I?

DENNIS: Er . . . I'm not quite sure, Wally, really. You could just put the area, I suppose.

WALLY: Are we having a biscuit?

DENNIS: D'you want one?

WALLY: Do you?

DENNIS: It all depends on what we've got left. [*He rummages around in the carrier bag and brings out half a packet of Marie biscuits.*] There's a few of the Marie biscuits left. Gone a bit stale, though.

WALLY: That's all right. I was only gonna dip 'em in me tea.

DENNIS: The ones at the top are all in bits and pieces.

WALLY: Never mind. You used to be able to go out and buy a pound of broken biscuits.

DENNIS: Well, you can't any more.

WALLY: I know you can't. I was just saying.

[KIERAN *comes running back into the lounge with* CYRIL *chasing after him.* WALLY *and* DENNIS *nudge each other.*]

DENNIS: I never saw Kieran come out, did you?

WALLY: No.

DENNIS: We'll have to start stocking up again this week. [*He rummages about in the carrier bag.*] Oh, hang on. There's a Bandit down the bottom here. D'you want it?

WALLY: Do you?

DENNIS: I'll just break a little bit off. [*He breaks a bit off, tastes it and pulls a face.*] Not all that exciting really, are they? I don't know. I never know what to get for the best.

WALLY: You know I'm not fussy, Dennis. As long

as you don't get no more of them whatsnames. Mussolini.

DENNIS: Who?

WALLY: Whatyoucall. Mantovani. You know. The
ones with all the currants.

DENNIS: Oh, I know the ones you mean. Garibaldi.

WALLY: That's right. I knew it was something
Italian.

DENNIS: I wasn't all that keen on them myself.

[CYRIL *catches* KIERAN *and takes
him off to the dormitory.*]

Have a fag.

WALLY: No, it's all right, Dennis. I'll have a roll-up.

DENNIS: Go on. I've got plenty.

WALLY: I'd like to cut down myself, really. But you
can't very well in here. Not with everyone
else fagging away.

[TREVOR *walks past.*]

DENNIS: Well, I don't intend to cut down. No. The
sooner I get to the cemetery the better off I'll
be.

WALLY: I was thinking of being cremated myself. Is
he still alive, d'you know?

DENNIS: Who?

WALLY: Whatsisname. You know. Gary . . .

DENNIS: Garibaldi. No, he's dead, lucky sod.

WALLY: What was he famous for?

DENNIS: He was a singer as far as I know.

WALLY: Oh, was he?

DENNIS: Yeah.

WALLY: You know them round ones, Dennis?
They're a bit like a shortbread only they're
not quite so sweet. They're more sweet than
the Marie ones, though. And they've got
these little whatsnames all over 'em.
Knobbles. D'you know the ones I mean?

11

[VICKY *comes out of the female dormitory with* JANET.]

DENNIS: No, I can't say I do. I'll have a look out, though. They generally have a picture on the packet. Oh, hello, Vicky.

VICKY: Janet, this is Dennis. And Wally.

DENNIS: How do you do.

WALLY: Pleased to meet you.

[TREVOR *walks past.*]

VICKY: Oh, and this is Trevor. Trevor, this is Janet.

TREVOR: Hello.

[TREVOR *walks off.*]

VICKY: Would you like to sit down here with Dennis and Wally for now? I'll come and see you a bit later on.

[DENNIS *and* WALLY *move up to each end of the couch, leaving* JANET *to sit down in the middle.*]

DENNIS: Like a cup of tea, dear?

JANET: Oh, yes please. Thank you very much.

WALLY: I'll get you one.

DENNIS: No, I'll get it.

WALLY: It's my turn, Dennis. D'you fancy another yourself?

DENNIS: I wouldn't say no.

[WALLY *goes off with the cups.*]

The kitchen's just out there. You can help yourself to tea and coffee any time you like.

JANET: I don't know for sure if I'll be staying yet.

DENNIS: Oh, I see.

JANET: I don't think I like the look of the place. It's not what I imagined.

DENNIS: You soon get used to it.

JANET: How long have you been here?

DENNIS: Er . . . Oooh . . . About four or five weeks, I think. I'm not quite sure.

12

[TREVOR *walks past and kicks the furniture.*]

JANET: What's wrong with that man?

DENNIS: Trevor? Oh, he wants a drink, that's all.

JANET: Couldn't he go and get a cup of tea?

DENNIS: He don't want a cup of tea. He's an alcoholic.

JANET: Oh, blimey. Are there a lot of them like that in here?

DENNIS: Oh yes, we've got about half a dozen on this ward.

JANET: He wouldn't kick another patient, would he?

DENNIS: Oh no. He's quite a nice person when you get to know him.

[*There is a sound of breaking crockery.* JANET *jumps.*]

JANET: What's that?

DENNIS: Sounds like somebody's had an accident out in the kitchen.

[WALLY *comes in with three cups of tea.*]

What's happening out there?

WALLY: It's that woman having a go again. Whatsername. The one with the big knockers. Oh, I beg your pardon.

DENNIS: Edna, you mean?

WALLY: That's the one. Vicky give her a telling off for dumping a pile of dishes in the sink. So she took 'em out of the sink again and chucked 'em on the floor. You're supposed to wash your dishes up after you. But some of 'em seem to think it's beneath their dignity.

[DENNIS *gets the sugar out of the carrier bag.*]

DENNIS: It's best to have your own supply of sugar. There is supposed to be sugar out in the kitchen but it keeps on disappearing all the time.

JANET: I don't suppose there's any brown sugar out there.

WALLY: Oh, whatsname, you mean.

DENNIS: Demerara.

WALLY: No, they don't have none of that. Just the ordinary Tate and Lyle.

JANET: Oh well. Never mind.

WALLY: By the way, Janet, you can help yourself to tea and coffee any time you like.

DENNIS: Yeah, I told her.

WALLY: The only trouble is, though, the milk keeps running out. Twenty-four pints they have delivered every morning but it never lasts out the whole day.

DENNIS: By rights you should be able to have a cup of Bournvita of a night-time. But it's not very often you get the chance.

WALLY: Some of 'em are just plain greedy. Especially the alcernolics. I've seen one or two of 'em drinking it glass after glass.

DENNIS: I reckon the nurses walk off with it, myself.

WALLY: We've tried keeping our own out here. But it soon goes off, what with the heat.

DENNIS: Help yourself to a biscuit, Janet.

JANET: Oh, no thanks, I mustn't.

WALLY: Watching your weight, eh?

JANET: No, it's not that. I never eat biscuits. They're bad for your teeth.

WALLY: Are they? Oh well, we don't have to worry about that, do we, Dennis?

DENNIS: What d'you mean? I haven't got false teeth.

WALLY: Oh, sorry. I thought you had. I could have

14

          sworn you said they wasn't all your own.

DENNIS: You never heard me say that.

WALLY: Oh. I must have got it wrong. I thought you said something about them being made specially out of porcelain.

DENNIS: I might have been talking about me crowns. That's not the same thing as false teeth, though.

WALLY: Oh, I see.

DENNIS: No, I don't think you do, Wally. I've got me own teeth underneath. The dentist files your own teeth down and sticks the crowns on top.

WALLY: I've never heard of that before.

DENNIS: Well, it's common knowledge. Mind you, they don't generally do it on the National Health. I had to go private and pay a fortune.

WALLY: I wasn't trying to show you up, Dennis.

DENNIS: That's all right. But you just want to get your facts right in the future. [*to* JANET] These are our own biscuits, these are. But there's bread out there in case you ever fancy making yourself a sandwich.

WALLY: There's cheese out there and all. And marmalade.

DENNIS: And we've got our own jam in here. Blackcurrant. Don't be frightened to ask if you ever want a lend of it.

WALLY: But don't leave it out in the kitchen. It'll vanish if you do.

DENNIS: Never leave anything of your own out there. The first week I was here I left a cucumber out in the fridge. I thought it would last a few days. Be nice to have the odd slice in a cheese sandwich. But it walked. We never found out who took it. You'd have thought somebody would have noticed a person walking out of there with a big green thing like that. But no.

WALLY: Mind you, there's all sorts wandering in and out. People off other wards. Visitors. Ex-patients. There's nothing to stop them helping theirselves to anything they see.

DENNIS: Fifteen loaves of bread we have delivered every day. Ten white ones and five Hovis. You'd think it'd be enough to go round but it never is. There's one bloke you have to watch — Michael.

WALLY: He likes to feed the birds.

DENNIS: See them French windows leading out to the garden. If you ever see a bloke walking out through there with a loaf of bread under his arm, tell one of the nurses.

WALLY: You can always tell he's been at it when you see all the crusts lying about on the grass. Like a load of little picture frames. I can't point him out to you just now. He's down at O.T.

DENNIS: That's Occupational Therapy.

WALLY: Where we should be by rights.

DENNIS: We thought we'd give it a miss today.

WALLY: They don't like it if you don't go. But they can't very well force you to go if you don't want to.

DENNIS: We go to Pottery ourselves. They show you how to make ashtrays. And vases. A bit on the messy side. Or you can do other things. Like painting and carpentry.

WALLY: She won't want to do Carpentry, will you?

DENNIS: They'll have you roped in for something in a day or two. Oh. Here she comes with the wages.

[VICKY *comes in with a box of brown wage packets. She hands a packet to* DENNIS, WALLY *and* TREVOR.]

VICKY: Janet, I'll get the Social Worker to come and see you later.

[JANET *nods.* VICKY *goes off.*]

JANET: Don't tell me you get paid for being in here.

DENNIS: No. It's pocket money.

JANET: Pocket money? What about sickness benefit?

DENNIS: We've used it all up. We've gone on to Social Security. They pay your rent and the hospital gives you something to spend.

WALLY: It don't go far. By the time you get your bits and pieces. Your washing powder. Your morning paper. And your cigarettes of course. This place makes you smoke. You'd think they'd try and put a stop to it, being doctors.

DENNIS: They daren't or they might have a riot on their hands.

[*He brings out his cigarettes.*]

Would you like one?

JANET: Er . . . No thanks.

[DENNIS *lights a cigarette.* WALLY *starts to roll one.*]

Yes, I will have one. Thank you very much. I brought about ten in with me. But I sat and smoked the whole lot while I was waiting to see the doctor.

DENNIS: Which one did you see?

JANET: I can't remember his name. Quite young. Short hair.

WALLY: Was he wearing a brown corduroy jacket?

JANET: Yeah, that's right.

WALLY: That'd be Wilson. We have him. He never

takes that jacket off from one day to the next.

DENNIS: Did you notice all the dandruff on his shoulders?

JANET: Yes I did as a matter of fact. You couldn't help but notice. I wonder if he realises.

DENNIS: Makes you feel sick, don't it. He's only been here a few weeks. Come about the same time as me. How long have I been here?

WALLY: I don't know. Four or five weeks, I suppose.

DENNIS: It must be getting on for that.

WALLY: None of 'em stay very long. You just get used to one, then somebody else comes in and takes over.

JANET: I don't suppose there's anywhere I could get some cigarettes.

WALLY: There is a little shop down the corridor.

DENNIS: Not much good, though. They only have a few brands. Have a couple of these for now and I'll get you some when I go out. I'll be going to MacMarket a bit later.

JANET: Are you allowed to go down the shops?

DENNIS: Course you are. You can go anywhere you like. Unless they said you couldn't.

JANET: They didn't say anything at all. I just thought if you were in hospital you'd have to stay inside.

DENNIS: Oh no. They like you to get out and about as much as you can.

WALLY: They won't let me out on my own, though.

DENNIS: No, but you can go out with a party. They took us on an outing the other Saturday. Up the Imperial War Museum.

WALLY: About six of us went with a couple of the nurses.

DENNIS: We didn't go round ourselves or have a look at any of the things.

WALLY: No. We sat in the cafeteria and had a cup of tea and a cake.

DENNIS: It was a nice ride out, though, wasn't it?

WALLY: Too many whatsnames in there for my liking.

DENNIS: Oh, the tourists, you mean.

WALLY: Yeah. And half of 'em was Jerries. Well, I mean to say, it don't seem right to me. I don't think it ought to be allowed.

JANET: I didn't think there'd be any outings. You know what I thought? I thought I was going to be put into a bed when I got in here.

DENNIS: Oh no, they don't like you stopping in bed. If anyone tries it on they soon have a gang of nurses round the bedside. 'Come on, get up. You'll feel better when you've had a nice shower.' Of course, if you're really ill they have to send you over to St Anthony's.

WALLY: Every now and then you get somebody taking an overdose. They shoot them over to St Anthony's for the stomach pump and the next day they're back in here again.

DENNIS: Mind you, there's nothing to stop you lying on the bed. As long as you get up and put your clothes on first. There's quite a few of 'em spend all day just lying on top of the bed. Mostly the women. A load of bloomin' miseries some of 'em.

WALLY: It strikes me women need more rest than men. You rarely see a woman come out before nine o'clock in the morning. The men are usually up and dressed and sitting out here by half-past seven.

DENNIS: If you see a man coming into your dormitory by the way, don't get alarmed. He'll only be coming in to have a bath.

19

WALLY: We've only got the showers in our dormitory. A shower's all very well. But I like to sit me bum in a bath at least once a week. We don't just walk in, though. We knock on the door first.

DENNIS: Anyone want another cup of tea?

WALLY: Oh, yes please.

JANET: That'd be nice.

[DENNIS *goes off with the cups.*]

WALLY: Shame about Dennis, really. Tried to do himself in. Took a dozen Panadol and turned on the oven.

JANET: I thought you couldn't kill yourself with the North Sea Gas.

WALLY: No, you can't. He woke up a few hours later. Thought to himself, I must have a cup of tea. Lit the gas under the kettle and boom! The whole kitchen went up. He was all right though, luckily. Only singed his hair. I'm not talking about him behind his back. It was all in the local paper. He'll show you the cutting if you ask him.

[TREVOR *walks past, muttering angrily to himself.*]

JANET: I don't like the look of that man. He's making me feel nervous.

WALLY: Oh, you don't want to let him worry you. He's all right.

JANET: I can't understand a word he's saying, can you?

WALLY: You can get the gist of it after a while. He's not daft or nothing like that. It's the drink that's done the damage. He plays the whatsname.

[*He mimes the saxophone.*]

JANET: What, the saxophone?

WALLY: Yeah. Used to be in a band, he reckons.

Semi-professional, like. He sometimes gives us a tune of an evening. Doesn't exactly get all the notes right. But we usually manage to have a bit of a sing-song.

[DENNIS *comes back with the tea.*]

She's worried about Trevor.

DENNIS: Oh, you don't want to take no notice. He's more scared of you than you are of him. Oh, look out, here comes trouble.

[DR WILSON *comes in and goes up to* WALLY.]

DR WILSON: Shall I see you now, Wally?

WALLY: Oh. Right.

[WALLY *picks up his tea and follows the doctor.*]

DENNIS: Er . . . Just between you and me, Janet, while I think of it. If you ever see Wally walking out on his own, tell one of the nurses quietly.

JANET: Why? He's not dangerous, is he?

DENNIS: No. Not exactly. But he can be a bit foul-mouthed. So don't go after him yourself if you do see him sneaking out. He has got out a couple of times. They had to inform the police. They soon found him the last time. In a Wimpy Bar. He reckons he can't remember nothing about it. It's the shock treatment makes him lose his memory.

JANET: What shock treatment? You don't mean electric shock, do you?

DENNIS: Yes, that's right.

JANET: Oh my God. I'm getting out of here.

[*She picks up her handbag.*]

DENNIS: No, it's all right. They don't give it to every-one. There's only a few of 'em have it. Wally's been having it for years, on and off. He reckons it makes a new man of him.

21

Must be something in it. He's always first in
the queue.

JANET: What's wrong with him?

DENNIS: He don't get on with his mother by all
accounts. She won't let him have no life of
his own. Leads him a proper dance. He
can't hold a job down because she don't
want him to leave the house. And when he
stops at home all day she nags him all the
while because he's not bringing in any
wages. He can't win. There's only the two
of them. He never knew who his father was.
When she goes he'll be all alone in the
world.

JANET: Oh dear.

SCENE TWO

The psychiatrist's office. DR WILSON *and*
WALLY *are sitting on chairs facing each*
other. WALLY *is drinking his tea.*

WALLY: I'm still putting on weight, Doctor. Mostly
round the whatsname. [*He pats his belly.*] I
reckon it must be the tablets what are doing
it.

DR WILSON: Have you been eating any more than usual?

WALLY: Oh no. I don't eat a lot. I mean, I like me
food all right but I'm not a pig. I'm
probably not getting enough exercise. I'd
feel a lot better if you'd let me go out. I'm
getting bored with having to wander round
the garden.

DR WILSON: How was the weekend at home?

WALLY: Well . . . She had to bring me back on the
Saturday night. She said I got in a temper
and called her an old cu . . . cu . . . I don't

like to say it in front of you. To tell you the truth, I don't remember saying it to her. But she insists I did. Huh. All I know was I was trying to listen to me records. Of course she thinks it's only background music. Talks her head off all the way through. I mean, I'm trying to follow Shirley Bassey. And she's keeping on about the sink being all blocked up. It's not my fault, is it? I'm in here. She's the one who gets it blocked up. I know for a fact she pushes baked beans down the plughole. And she washes her hair in the kitchen sink, filthy cow. I'm the one who's supposed to rake it out, though, oh yes. She can't go in the bathroom when she's on her own. Not since she saw that film. You know. The one where the woman runs off with all the money and stops at that motel. The blonde one. Used to be married to him who was in the film with Marilyn Monroe. Where he was dressed up in women's clothes. He was dressed up as a woman and all at the end. The one in the film I'm talking about, where whatsername gets stabbed in the shower. She said I shouldn't have let her watch it. Well, I told her not to watch it. Three times I warned her. She reckons she never heard me. She has to have a wash down in the kitchen every night. I wouldn't care but she uses the same bowl for the washing up. She tries to make out she uses a different one. Says she's got two the same colour. But I know for a fact there's only the one plastic bowl. The next time you talk to her you can tell her I wasn't born yesterday.

SCENE THREE

The lounge. DENNIS *and* JANET *are sitting on the couch.* TREVOR *is sitting on a chair. He is polishing his saxophone.*

JANET: I'm all alone in the world now.

DENNIS: You're not, are you?

JANET: Yes. My Mum and Dad are dead and I'm not married. So. . .

DENNIS: I'm all alone now, too, more or less. She's gone off and left me. The wife.

JANET: Oh no.

DENNIS: Yeah. She went off with one of me mates.

JANET: Oh, how rotten.

DENNIS: I can't understand it. We always got on very well.

JANET: I've never met anyone I've really got on with. Not really. If I'm attracted to them physically I'm usually not attracted to them emotionally. Or the other way round. There's always something that's not quite right. The last man I was involved with, he was a very nice person and really hand-some. But I just couldn't stand the way he talked. I know it wasn't his fault. He came from Birmingham. His voice used to go right through me. And he wasn't . . . Well, I don't think he'd had enough education. He seemed a bit ignorant about a lot of things. I know he couldn't help it. He'd had a lot of time off school when he was little. I didn't like to introduce him to my friends.

DENNIS: You always take a chance whoever you pick. My wife had the self-same back-ground as me. So did the bloke she went off with, come to think of it. He's much the same build as me and all. Same heighth.

Same age. Done the same job. Only where I worked me way up through experience, he had his City and Guilds Certificate. Maybe that's what impressed her, I don't know. It wouldn't be so bad if only she hadn't taken the girl. [*He gets a photograph out of his wallet.*] Look, there she is. My Susanna. She'll be thirteen come next February.

JANET: Oh, she looks like you, doesn't she.
   [DENNIS *bursts into tears.*]

DENNIS: Sorry to be like this.

JANET: That's all right. Don't worry.

DENNIS: I can't seem to stop myself. No matter how many pills I take, they don't do any good.

JANET: Have you ever gone all hot and cold?

DENNIS: Oh yes. Loads of times.

JANET: That's what happens to me. One minute I'm burning up and breaking out in a sweat and the next minute I'm freezing cold and shivering. The doctor says it's my nerves.

DENNIS: Yeah, that's what they reckon causes it.

JANET: He put me on Valium. I was all right for a couple of weeks and then one night I was just going off to sleep when I suddenly got this feeling in my stomach. A sinking sort of feeling. I turned on the light and do you know what? I couldn't see a thing. My eyesight had gone all blurred and there was a zigzag light sort of darting about in front of the left eye. I thought I was going blind. I had to call the doctor out. Lucky I knew his number off by heart. He said it was only my nerves again and he gave me some different tablets. They seemed to do some good for a while. But yesterday afternoon I started to go all hot and cold again. I went back to the doctor to see if he could give me something else. But he wouldn't. He wrote me out a letter to come up here. I don't think I should have been sent here, though. I think there's something wrong with me physically.

DENNIS: You probably need a rest. You ought to try and enjoy yourself while you're here.

JANET: Enjoy myself?

DENNIS: Perhaps we could go to the pictures one night.

JANET: Do they let you out at night?

DENNIS: Oh yes. You can stop out as late as you like. They lock the ward at eight o'clock but that's only to stop people off other wards from coming in. If you're late you just have to ring the bell.

JANET: Well . . . I don't know.

DENNIS: Or we could go in the afternoon if you prefer.

[WALLY *comes back into the lounge and sits down.*]

DENNIS: How did you get on?

WALLY: Not bad, you know. Same as usual really. He don't know what you're on about half the time.

DENNIS: I'd feel a lot happier if I saw him taking notes.

WALLY: He never writes nothing down.

DENNIS: No. It must all go in one ear and out the other.

TREVOR: He's a load of bleedin' old rubbish.

JANET: How often do you get to see the doctor?

DENNIS: Two or three times a week at first. Then it tails off to just the once a week.

WALLY: You can always have a chat to one of the nurses, though.

DENNIS: Yes, if you can manage to tell 'em apart

from the patients. I haven't got a lot of time for them myself.

WALLY: They're on to a cushy little number in here. Sitting about gossiping all day. Giggling among theirselves about their boyfriends.

DENNIS: They don't take the job a bit serious. One of the young ones come on duty the other morning straight from an all night party. She was staggering about all day with her eyes half closed.

WALLY: I feel more settled with the night staff myself.

DENNIS: They wear a uniform. You know where you are with them.

> [CYRIL *comes in and rings a handbell.*]

WALLY: Tablet time. We have to go and queue up at the counter.

> [DENNIS, TREVOR *and* WALLY *get up and go off.* KIERAN *comes out and goes off.* SYLVIA *and* OLIVE *come out of the female dormitory and go off.* VICKY *comes up to* JANET.]

VICKY: Janet, if you'd like to go up to the counter, they'll give you a Valium.

JANET: What for?

VICKY: Dr Wilson said you can have one three times a day if you need it.

JANET: I'm already taking some tablets three times a day.

VICKY: You gave them to Dr Wilson. D'you remember?

JANET: No I didn't. I let him have a look at them to see what they were. He gave them back to me. [*She looks in her handbag.*] I'm sure he

27

gave them back. No. He couldn't have done. They're not in here.

VICKY: We're not going to be giving you any more of those.

JANET: Oh, but you can't stop them just like that. My doctor said I mustn't stop taking them suddenly or I'd have some very bad side effects.

VICKY: Well, if you do you're in the best place to have them.

JANET: What? That's not very fair. What will I do if I get another one of those attacks?

VICKY: The Valium should help.

JANET: Oh no it won't. I've had them before. They don't do a thing for me. Honestly. I'm immune to them.

[*She stands up.*]

Look, I want my own tablets. You've got no right to take them away.

[DENNIS, WALLY *and* TREVOR *come back and sit down.*]

VICKY: Would you like to go and have a lie down?

JANET: No, I wouldn't. I want to see the doctor. Where is he?

VICKY: He's gone to lunch. Just sit down for a minute.

JANET: No. You leave me alone. [*She starts to cry.*] I thought you were going to do something to help me in here.

VICKY: The Valium is there if you want it.

[VICKY *goes off.*]

DENNIS: I'm only on Valium myself. Plus a Mogadon of a night-time. What was you taking before?

JANET: Motival. Little pink ones.

DENNIS: Oh I know. I've had them. Poor old Wally, he has to have Largactil.

WALLY: They make your stomach swell up something rotten.

DENNIS: Yours is not so bad. But there's a couple of fellows in here who look as if they're six months gone.

WALLY: You mustn't sit out in the sun while you're taking them, neither. Oh well. Coming down the canteen, Janet?

DENNIS: Hadn't you better warn her about the food?

WALLY: Yeah. It's terrible.

DENNIS: I don't go down of a dinnertime myself. I go to a little cafe down the road.

JANET: Oh. D'you get a choice in the canteen?

WALLY: No. But you can always have a salad if you don't like the look of the hot dinner.

JANET: I probably won't like it. I'm fussy about what I eat. I'm practically a vegetarian.

WALLY: Oh, are you?

JANET: Well, not a strict one. I do eat fish and I might have a pork chop sometimes. But only if I cook it myself.

WALLY: If you wanted to tell them you was a real vegetarian they might do something about it. There's a fellow in here, Melvin, Jewish chap, he has food brought in for him specially.

DENNIS: It don't look any better to me than what they serve up in the canteen. I generally have the breakfast and the supper down there. But I like to make sure of a proper meal at least once a day.

WALLY: There's one woman in here, she never goes down the canteen. Stays inside the dormitory all the time.

DENNIS: That's Olive. You'll see her come out to the kitchen four or five times a day for a marmalade sandwich.

29

WALLY: The trouble is, the National Health don't give so much money for food in a mental hospital.

JANET: This is not exactly a mental hospital, is it?

DENNIS: Course it is.

WALLY: What did you think it was?

JANET: I mean, it's not like a lunatic asylum. They don't have anybody raving mad in here.

DENNIS: Oh they do. Only they put them all together in the Mansion.

WALLY: That's the big house over the other side. They keep 'em under lock and key.

JANET: Oh, my God. Do they have padded cells and all that sort of thing?

DENNIS: Oh no. They all have separate bedrooms. Done up very smart. Divan beds. Reading lamps. Your own washbasin. And a nurse to every patient by the looks of it.

WALLY: One of the men off this ward got a transfer over there. We went to visit him. Well, more to have a look round, really. See what it was like. Very quiet. He didn't have a lot to say for himself. Not like when he was in here yelling and shouting. And looking up women's skirts. He's got a big black nurse watching over him now. Looks like a heavyweight champion.

DENNIS: They get waited on hand and foot over there.

JANET: It sounds as if it might be worth letting them think you're really round the bend.

WALLY: Yeah. Right, shall we go?
[*They all get up.*]

DENNIS: I'll see you later. D'you want me to get you anything down the shops?

JANET: Oh yes. Is there a health food store round here?

DENNIS: Oooh, I don't rightly know. I generally only go as far as Lavells. I'll have a look out though if you like.

JANET: It doesn't matter.

DENNIS: No, it's all right. What was it you wanted?

JANET: Some wheatgerm.

DENNIS: What was that?

JANET: Wheatgerm. It has to be the one in the jar, though. They do do one in a packet but that's not the one I have.

DENNIS: Oh, I see.

JANET: And d'you think you could get me some sugar? Brown sugar, I mean. It's called Barbados Muscavado.

DENNIS: I think I'll have to write that down.

> [DENNIS *writes it down on his cigarette packet.*]

JANET: And a bottle of Vitamin B pills.

DENNIS: What's that? B for Bertie?

JANET: Yes. You'll probably see a whole lot of different Vitamin Bs. The one I have is the Vitamin B Complex.

DENNIS: Right.

JANET: Oh and twenty Silk Cut King Size. No. I'd better have forty.

> [JANET *gives some money to* DENNIS. *They all go off.*]

SCENE FOUR

The female dormitory. OLIVE *is lying on the bed. She is eating a marmalade sandwich.* SYLVIA *is ironing and smoking.* JANET *comes in and sits on her bed.*

SYLVIA: Oh, hello. I've got such a pile of ironing. I keep putting it off till I've got nothing left to wear. Not that you have to bother in here.

| | But I've got to go out tonight. |

JANET: I've hardly brought anything with me.

SYLVIA: No, I didn't at first. But I had to keep on asking for more and more stuff to be brought in. I'll have to hire a removal van when I go.

JANET: How long have you been here?

SYLVIA: Seven weeks.

JANET: I don't think I'll last out more than one day. They've taken away my tablets and I haven't had a thing to eat. I went down the canteen, took one look at the food and came straight out again.

SYLVIA: Disgusting, isn't it. I don't usually bother, apart from Friday. Fish and chips. The rest of the week, yuk! You can help yourself to bread and cheese in the kitchen if you want.

JANET: There's somebody out there at the moment. Making himself an omelette.

SYLVIA: You wanna shove him out the way.

JANET: He's doing himself a side salad as well, though. He's got all his lettuce and tomato and his celery and radishes spread out all over the place. D'you think I could possibly borrow a cigarette? I can give it back to you later. Somebody's gone out to get me some.

SYLVIA: On my locker. Help yourself. I'll have one as well.

JANET: I wish I could cut down.

SYLVIA: Yeah, so do I.

JANET: I did get down to ten. But as soon as I knew I had to come in here it went up to twenty again. I didn't really think they'd actually want me to come in. I thought I was only going to be an out-patient. I don't think I should have come in. I was better off just going to my doctor and getting tablets off him. She said I could have a Valium. That Vicky woman. I didn't take it though. I wouldn't give her the satisfaction. There's something about her I don't trust. I don't think she likes me either. I can tell. Valium's no good to me. I've had them before. They don't do a thing for me. Perhaps I should have taken it though. I'm starting to feel a bit shaky.

SYLVIA: You can have one of mine if you like. I've got loads.

JANET: Oh. D'you think I should?

SYLVIA: Of course. They said you should have one, didn't they?

JANET: All right then.

SYLVIA: You'd better have half a dozen. They're only two milligram. I hope they haven't gone stale. I've had them for ages.

> [SYLVIA *takes a bottle out of her handbag and gives a handful of pills to* JANET.]

JANET: Thank you very much. What do they give you in here?

SYLVIA: Amitryptilin. I wouldn't recommend them, though. They affect your balance. And you wake up in the morning with slurred speech. At least I do.

JANET: I'm going to tell that Dr Wilson I want my tablets back when I see him.

SYLVIA: Yes, you want to tell him. You have to stand up for yourself in here.

> [SYLVIA *stands the iron up on its end while she folds up a piece of clothing.*]

OLIVE: You mind that iron!

SYLVIA: Yes, all right.

OLIVE: You'll be sorry if it slips. I knew a woman who dropped an iron on her foot.

SYLVIA: Oh, leave off.

OLIVE: It came up in a great big blister. She never had it seen to. And when it burst the germs got in. And the poison spread all the way up her leg.

> [SYLVIA *slams the iron down. There is a tap on the door.*]

SYLVIA: Come in.

> [BRIAN *comes in. He is carrying several bags.*]

Oh, hello.

BRIAN: Hello, luv.

> [BRIAN *kisses* SYLVIA.]

OLIVE: Huh.

BRIAN: I've got you some of that taramasalata from t'takeaway.

SYLVIA: Oh, good.

> [SYLVIA *unplugs the iron and folds up the ironing board.*]

BRIAN: You'd better eat it right away while t'bread's still hot. [*to* JANET] I'm trying to fatten her up.

SYLVIA: Oh Brian, this is Janet.

BRIAN: Hello, luv. Just come in today, have you?

JANET: Yes.

BRIAN: It's not so bad. You'll soon settle in.

SYLVIA: D'you want some of this, Janet?

JANET: No, it's all right, thanks.

SYLVIA: She hasn't had any lunch.

JANET: I didn't like the look of it.

SYLVIA: See, I told you it wasn't just me.

BRIAN: I've washed your tee shirts for you. And the two pair of slacks. I didn't get round to t'dress because it wants doing by hand. I'll do it tonight. You'd better hang these slacks up. They're dry but they want to be aired.

SYLVIA: That's more bleedin' ironing.

BRIAN: Well you know I'd iron them for you, luv, but they'd only get creased up again bringing them on t'tube and having to take them in to work with me before I can bring them in here. Oh. I had a look round t'market before I came in and I got you some of these.

> [BRIAN *opens up his bags and brings out a pile of brightly coloured nylon knickers, lace-trimmed and fairly large.*]

They were only 25p a pair.

SYLVIA: Huh. I'm not surprised.

BRIAN: Or three pair for 70p. So I got you half a dozen.

SYLVIA: They're a bit on the big side, aren't they?

BRIAN: I don't think they are. They're not too big, are they, Janet?

JANET: Er . . . No. I shouldn't think so.

BRIAN: They're ordinary women's size.

SYLVIA: You could have asked me first.

BRIAN: I would have done only they were all queuing up. I thought they'd have all been gone if I left it too late. They're over a pound a pair in t'British Home Stores, you know.

SYLVIA: Yes, all right. Don't keep on.

BRIAN: D'you want them, then?

SYLVIA: Yes, I might as well. Nobody's going to see them in here.

BRIAN: You don't have to have them if you don't want them. What d'you think, Janet? They're all right, aren't they?

JANET: Yes, they're very nice.

35

BRIAN: You'd wear them, wouldn't you?

JANET: Er . . . Yes. I probably would.

BRIAN: Well, if Sylvia doesn't want them, you could always have them if they're any good to you. I wouldn't want t'money for them or owt like that. I just don't like to think of them going to waste.

OLIVE: I'll have them.

BRIAN: Oh. Well . . . I mean, are you sure? I mean, I don't think . . .

OLIVE: I'm not as big as I look.

SYLVIA: I said I'm having them, didn't I?

OLIVE: She won't wear them.

SYLVIA: Oh yes I will. What's it got to do with her?

BRIAN: You could have a couple of pair each if you like.

OLIVE: I'll have the red ones.

BRIAN: Oh. Well, I'll leave you to sort it out amongst yourselves.

[BRIAN *sits down on* SYLVIA'*s bed.*]

How have you been today?

SYLVIA: Bloody awful.

[JANET *gets up.*]

JANET: I think I'll go and get myself some cheese toast.

BRIAN: I'll see you again, luv.

[JANET *goes out.*]

SCENE FIVE

The lounge. WALLY *is sitting on the couch.* KIERAN *is sitting in an armchair. There are two cups of tea on the table and another cup with the saucer on top of it.* JANET *comes in with a cup of tea and a slice of cheese on toast. She sits on the couch.*

WALLY: Oh, hello there.

JANET: I've got myself some cheese on toast.

WALLY: [*to* KIERAN] She didn't have no dinner.
[KIERAN *tuts.*]
Oh Janet, this is Kieran. Janet come in this morning.

KIERAN: Hello there. [*He winks.*] When's your night out?

JANET: What?

WALLY: He's only pulling your leg. It's not often we get a good-looking girl in here.

JANET: Oh.

> [DENNIS *comes in with a Mac-Market carrier bag and a 'Heath and Heather' carrier bag. He takes out the wheatgerm, the sugar and the vitamins.*]

DENNIS: [*to* JANET] Is this what you wanted?

JANET: Oh yes. Thank you very much.

DENNIS: There is a health food store a little bit further down. Next door to Freeman Hardy and Willis. Self-service. I had to hunt around a bit. Funny sort of a smell in there. I couldn't put a name to it. I hope these are the right Vitamin B.

JANET: Yes, they are. Thanks a lot.

DENNIS: There's your fags. And here's your change.

WALLY: Your tea's there, Dennis.

DENNIS: Oh, ta. I got us some Jaffa Cakes.

WALLY: Oh good.

DENNIS: And I got a packet of digestive. I couldn't see any sign of them knobbly ones, Wally. I did have a look.

WALLY: Never mind. Perhaps I've got it wrong. I might have just imagined them. What did you have for dinner?

DENNIS: I had a pizza.

WALLY: Oh, did you?

DENNIS: Yeah.

WALLY: What are they like, them?

DENNIS: They're all right now and again. What did you have?

WALLY: We had toad in the hole, mashed potatoes and peas. I could have done with another sausage myself. Still . . .

JANET: I couldn't face it.

WALLY: She didn't like the look of the salads, neither.

DENNIS: Oh, you must eat, Janet. They weigh you once a week, you know.

JANET: What for?

WALLY: To make sure you're not starving to death.

DENNIS: It gives the nurses something to do.

WALLY: She had some cheese on toast. [*to* KIERAN] Janet's a whatsname.

DENNIS: Vegetarian.

KIERAN: Is that a fact?

JANET: Well, sort of. I don't eat meat very often.

KIERAN: You'll have no blood inside of you if you don't eat meat, dear. It'll all turn to water.

JANET: I get enough iron from all the other things I eat. See this? [*She holds up the jar of wheat-germ.*] It's full of iron.

KIERAN: What's that at all?

JANET: Wheatgerm. D'you want a taste?
[*They all have a taste and pull faces.*]

WALLY: Oh no.

DENNIS: I don't think much of that, I'm afraid.

KIERAN: Oh, Jesus, I've been poisoned.
[KIERAN *coughs and splutters.*]

JANET: Are you all right?

WALLY: He's pulling your leg again.

WALLY: I must go for a sit down. You got the er . . . ?

[DENNIS *brings an orange toilet roll out of the communal carrier bag and passes it discreetly to* WALLY *who holds it up to* JANET.]

This is what you wanna get yourself. I wouldn't advise using the stuff out there.

[WALLY *goes off.*]

DENNIS: You don't want to use the soap out there, neither. It takes all the skin off your hands.

KIERAN: Here's my wife coming in now.

DENNIS: You know you can have visitors any time you like. As long as they're out by eight o'clock at night. I don't have any myself. A few of 'em come up at first with bunches of grapes and bottles of after-shave. But once they realise you're not in bed they soon stop bothering.

[MRS O'TOOLE *comes walking in very slowly with a very heavy shopping bag. She pulls up a chair, sits down and groans.*]

MRS O'TOOLE: [*to* KIERAN] How are you? Are you all right?

KIERAN: D'you hear what she's asking? Am I all right. Of course I'm not all right. If I was all right I wouldn't be in here.

MRS O'TOOLE: Ah, shut up. How are you, Dennis?

DENNIS: Not so bad, thanks.

MRS O'TOOLE: [*to* JANET] I haven't seen you before, have I?

DENNIS: Oh no. This is Janet. She came in today.

JANET: Hello.

MRS O'TOOLE: How do you do. [*to* KIERAN] I got you a bottle of Lucozade.

KIERAN: I've two bottles of that stuff inside.

MRS O'TOOLE: Well, now you've three. And here's a dirty book for you. Somebody left it behind on the bus.

KIERAN: Why didn't you hand it in?

MRS O'TOOLE: Ah, it's only an old paperback.

KIERAN: Somebody might be looking for it.

MRS O'TOOLE: Well, they're not going to find it, are they?

KIERAN: *Seventy-Nine Park Avenue*. Complete and unexpurgated.

> [WALLY *comes back, sits down and puts the toilet roll back in the carrier bag.*]

WALLY: Hello.

MRS O'TOOLE: Hello, Wally. [*to* KIERAN] And there's a pound of bananas for you.

KIERAN: Bananas? What do you think I am — a monkey? I might as well be locked up in the zoo.

DENNIS: Would you like a cup of tea, Mrs O'Toole?

MRS O'TOOLE: That's very nice of you. Thank you, Dennis.

DENNIS: Anybody else want a refill?

JANET: Yes please.

WALLY: I might as well.

KIERAN: Thanks.

> [DENNIS *goes off with the cups.*]

MRS O'TOOLE: Why didn't you offer to make me a cup of tea?

KIERAN: I didn't know you wanted a cup.

> [KIERAN *flicks through the book.* MRS O'TOOLE *gets out her knitting.*]

MRS O'TOOLE: I haven't sat down all day. I took all the net curtains down first thing this morning, washed them out and put them up again. That step ladder wants to be seen to. I nearly broke me neck coming down. I took the blankets off the bed and left them soaking in the bath. I'll have to rinse them out and hang them up as soon as I get home. I cleaned all the windows but only the inside.

I wouldn't attempt to do the outside.
They're black but I don't know who's going
to do them. You can't get a man these days
to clean a window for you. I washed down
every bit of the paintwork. D'you know, the
bedroom is crying out for a coat of
emulsion. I was looking at the price of
paint in Woolworth. It's gone up an awful
lot. But even if I could afford it, how would
I carry it home? I'd have to be running up
and down the road with one can at a time.

KIERAN: [*reading*]'She put the towel down and
rubbed her face vigorously, then under her
arms and across her body. She put the towel
back on the chair and reached behind her
for her brassiere.'

MRS O'TOOLE: Put out your hand till I measure this sleeve.

[KIERAN *sticks out his arm.*]

A couple of inches more. I wonder, will I
have enough wool?

[DENNIS *comes back with the tea.*]

KIERAN: I hope you're going to be making them the
same length this time. The last one had to
have one of the cuffs turned back as far as
the elbow.

MRS O'TOOLE: There's nothing wrong with the sleeve. It
must be one of your arms that's longer than
the other.

JANET: Here's the doctor coming again.

[DR WILSON *comes in and goes up to*
DENNIS.]

DR WILSON: Shall I see you now, Dennis?

[DENNIS *gets up.*]

JANET: Could I have a word with you, Doctor?

DR WILSON: Er . . . Yes. Shall I see you later?

[DR WILSON *goes off with* DENNIS.]

KIERAN: [*reading*] 'She slipped out of her housecoat and sat down in front of a vanity table. She wore nothing but a strapless brassiere, panties and long silk stockings that were secured to a tiny garter belt around her waist. She gazed at him mischievously. "Excuse the working clothes."' This is a good book, this is.

MRS O'TOOLE: It's a lot of old filth. Couldn't you read it to yourself?

WALLY: I'll have a lend of it, Kieran, when you've finished it.

KIERAN: You can blame my wife for corrupting the two of us.

SCENE SIX
The psychiatrist's office. DR WILSON *and* DENNIS *are sitting facing each other.*

DR WILSON: How are you feeling, Dennis?

DENNIS: I don't know, really. All right, I suppose.

DR WILSON: You're sleeping all right?

DENNIS: Yeah, not bad.

DR WILSON: Eating well?

DENNIS: Yes, I am as a matter of fact. I wouldn't be, though, if I had to rely on hospital food.
[DR WILSON *smiles.*]

DR WILSON: You've been getting out and about a bit more?

DENNIS: Only down the shops. I generally get the bits and pieces for the others. Oh, yes, and I might be going to the pictures one night this week.

DR WILSON: Good. The more you get out and enjoy yourself, the better. Have you thought any more about what you're going to do when you leave here?

DENNIS: Er . . . No. Not much.

DR WILSON: You'll be going back to the same job, will you?

DENNIS: I suppose so. I don't much fancy going back there, though. Not with everyone knowing about me wife and that. He's still working there. The fellow she went off with. I know he's in another department, but still . . .

DR WILSON: Why haven't you looked for another job if you feel like that?

DENNIS: I couldn't get another job. Not for the same money. If anyone ought to be getting another job it ought to be him.

DR WILSON: You should be ready to start work again quite soon.

DENNIS: I don't see how I can. Not if I keep on bursting into tears every couple of hours.

DR WILSON: I think you should be ready to go home on Friday week.

DENNIS: What? Go home for good, you mean?

DR WILSON: You've been here for ten weeks now, Dennis.

DENNIS: I can't have been.

DR WILSON: You came in on the 10th of July.

DENNIS: Are you sure?

DR WILSON: Yes. I'm quite sure. Now what about last weekend? You were going to spend it at home. Why didn't you go?

DENNIS: I did.

DR WILSON: No you didn't. You went to the Imperial War Museum.

DENNIS: I know I did. But I went home on the Sunday morning. At least I made the journey. Sat down. Stared at the four walls. I can't stop there on me own.

DR WILSON: You could get somebody to share with you.

DENNIS: Who?

DR WILSON: People are always looking for somewhere to live. You could advertise.

DENNIS: No thanks. I don't want a lot of Pakistanis coming round. You can't say no to them nowadays.

DR WILSON: Couldn't you go and stay with one of your relations for a while?

DENNIS: No. Nobody wants me staying with them. I'm too much of a bleedin' liability. Why do I have to go? There's plenty of 'em been in here a lot longer than me.

DR WILSON: You will be coming back as an out-patient.

DENNIS: What's the good of that? You haven't done nothing for me while I've been in here.

DR WILSON: What do you expect me to do for you, Dennis?

DENNIS: I don't know, do I? You must be able to do something.

DR WILSON: I can't wave a magic wand.

DENNIS: I thought this was supposed to be a psychiatric hospital. For all the psychiatry you've done on me I might as well be staying at Butlins. You haven't even told me what's wrong with me.

DR WILSON: I've told you what I think you should do. It's up to you to get on with it.

DENNIS: Well, I will. I will. I'll get myself organised if you'll just let me stay a little bit longer.

DR WILSON: We're short of beds, Dennis.

DENNIS: What if I went private and paid for a bed? I've got a few bob put aside.

DR WILSON: We don't have any private patients here.

DENNIS: Well, you know what I'll do if I have to go back there. I'll do what I done before. I've got a cupboard full of tablets at home, you know. I've got tranquillizers, pain-killers,

anti-depressants, antibiotics. I'll swallow
the whole lot in one go.

DR WILSON: I'll see you again in a few days, Dennis.

DENNIS: Oh no you won't. I want to see somebody
higher up. You're not a proper psychiatrist.
I can't talk to you. None of the others can,
neither. We all think you're nothing but a
posh little twerp.

> [DENNIS *jumps up, takes a 50p piece
> out of his pocket and slams it down
> on the table.*]

There you are. That's for you. Go down the
chemist and buy yourself a bottle of Vosene.
And while you're down there leave that
corduroy jacket in the cleaner's.

> [DENNIS *storms out.*]

SCENE SEVEN

The lounge. WALLY *is sitting on the couch
with* JANET. KIERAN *is asleep.* MRS O'TOOLE
is knitting. TREVOR *is pacing up and down.*

MRS O'TOOLE: The dining-room wants redecorating. I'll
have to do it myself. He's never been able to
turn his hand to anything round the house.
He might hold the ladder for me while I'm
painting the ceiling.

WALLY: I could do the whole lot for you in a
fortnight. I done everything in our house.
Knocked down the living-room wall. Made
it all into one big room. Panelled over all
the doors . . .

MRS O'TOOLE: Isn't your mother a lucky woman.

WALLY: No. She doesn't think so.

MRS O'TOOLE: Of course she does. If I had somebody to do
all that you'd never hear a cross word out of

me. I've only myself to blame, of course. I knew what he was like when I married him. The father was bone idle. The poor mother worked herself into the grave at fifty-three. She had nine boys, God rest her soul, and none of them would ever lift a finger. They'd be too busy sitting round the fire discussing politics. All the brothers are the same, except the one that went into the priesthood and he has a housekeeper running round after him.

[DENNIS *comes in and sits down.*]

WALLY: How did you get on?

DENNIS: Oh, fine. Absolutely marvellous. I've got to go home next week.

WALLY: Oh, really? Oh dear. Well, I won't half miss you, Dennis. But it's probably all for the best.

[DENNIS *bursts into tears.*]

DENNIS: Sorry. I'm sorry. Don't take any notice of me.

MRS O'TOOLE: Would you like a cup of tea, Dennis?

WALLY: Or shall we have coffee for a change?

DENNIS: I don't want nothing!

[DENNIS *sweeps everything off the table and starts kicking the table in. Everyone jumps out of the way, except* KIERAN, *who is still asleep.*]

WALLY: Vicky! Vicky!

[VICKY *comes running up.*]

VICKY: What's the matter, Dennis?

[DENNIS *sobs.* VICKY *puts her arm round him.*]

D'you want to tell me about it?

[DENNIS *nods.*]

Come on then.

46

[VICKY *and* DENNIS *go off. The others start clearing up the mess, except* KIERAN.]

WALLY: They always do something like that. Every time somebody's told to go, they have a tantrum.

MRS O'TOOLE: The poor man. They've no right to be sending him home. He isn't anywhere near to being cured.

WALLY: I've never seen anyone go out of here cured.

[CYRIL *comes in with a broom and a dustpan and brush.*]

MRS O'TOOLE: Hello, Cyril. How are you?

CYRIL: I'm fine, thanks, Mrs O'Toole. How are you today?

MRS O'TOOLE: To tell you the truth, Cyril, I'm not well at all. I don't want to let on to Kieran but I've been getting an awful lot of indigestion. I wonder what's the best thing to take for it?

CYRIL: Take two Rennies three times a day after meals.

MRS O'TOOLE: I've tried them things and they give me the flatulence. I think it might be psychological indigestion. I can't help getting depressed with him the way he is. How has he been behaving himself?

CYRIL: He had a little run out this morning but he didn't get very far.

MRS O'TOOLE: I suppose he took all the clothes off him again.

CYRIL: Most of them.

MRS O'TOOLE: Oh God, I'm so ashamed. Why does he do it? I can't figure it out at all. I wonder what is he trying to tell us?

[CYRIL *shrugs and shakes his head.*]

CYRIL: Don't worry, Mrs O'Toole. Have you tried any Milk of Magnesia?

MRS O'TOOLE: Oh, the white stuff. I'll get myself a bottle of that on the way home. I'd better be going. Wake up and say goodbye to me, will you?
[*She wakes* KIERAN *up.* CYRIL *goes off.*]

KIERAN: Ah. What do you want?

MRS O'TOOLE: I'm going home.

KIERAN: Are you?

MRS O'TOOLE: I am. Goodbye now.
[*She gives him a kiss on the cheek and goes off.* CYRIL *comes back in.*]

CYRIL: [*to* JANET] Would you like a game of table tennis, Janet?

JANET: No thanks. I don't go in for that sort of thing.

CYRIL: What about having a game of Scrabble? You could have a game with us, Wally.

WALLY: No. Not just now, thanks, Cyril.

CYRIL: [*to* JANET] You getting on all right?

JANET: Yes, I'm OK. Would it be all right if I went out for a few minutes?

CYRIL: Yes. You can go out.

JANET: I just want to get an *Evening Standard.*

CYRIL: That's all right.

JANET: [*to* WALLY] D'you want a paper or anything?

WALLY: Er. . . Well, Dennis usually gets the evening paper. He might be offended. You know . . .

JANET: Yes, all right.
[JANET *goes off.*]

SCENE EIGHT

The female dormitory. OLIVE *is lying on her bed with a pack of cards spread out in front of her.* SYLVIA *is getting dressed to go out. Her bed is littered with a variety of garments. She puts on a dress, looks at herself, takes it off and puts on a very tight low-necked blouse and a pair of velvet trousers. The zip will not do up so she lies on the bed, breathes in and pulls up the zip. She stands up, breathes out, pulls down the zip, takes the trousers off and puts on a pair of jeans.* JANET *comes in with an* Evening Standard. *She sits down on her bed.*

SYLVIA: I was going to wear a dress but I feel happier in the jeans somehow. I wish I knew where we were going, though. Perhaps I ought to wear the satin ones in case we're going anywhere flash.

> [*She takes off the jeans and puts on a pair of satin trousers.*]

Does this top go with these trousers?

JANET: Oh yes.

> [SYLVIA *struggles into a pair of very high-heeled glittery boots. She stands up.*]

SYLVIA: Oh Christ. They're too short with these boots. I'll have to tuck them in.

> [*She tucks the trousers into the boots.*]

Does that look all right?

JANET: Yes, it looks nice.

SYLVIA: Oh, I don't know. I think I ought to wear a dress in case we go somewhere respectable. I wish he'd done that dress for me. I ought to have washed it myself. If you want to do any washing, by the way, there is a laundry. Only there's a permanent queue down there and they're always fighting and arguing. What some of them do is hang their

washing up in the shower. It's usually dry
by the morning. Only don't leave nothing
good out there. Things have been known to
walk off in the middle of the night.

> [SYLVIA *starts to put on her make-
> up. A handbell rings.*]

Tablet time. I'll have to be going soon. Are
you having a Valium this time?

JANET: I think I'd better have one. I wonder what
strength they're going to give me.

SYLVIA: They usually give five milligram during
the day.

JANET: That might not be enough for me.

SYLVIA: You can always have some more of mine.

JANET: Thanks.

> [*They go off.* OLIVE *gets up and goes
> off.*]

SCENE NINE

The lounge. Night-time. TREVOR *is playing
'On the Sunny Side of the Street' on his
saxophone. The* NIGHT NURSE *comes in,
pauses, joins in the singing for a few
moments, then goes into the female
dormitory.*

SCENE TEN

The female dormitory. JANET *is lying on
her bed in her dressing-gown. She is
reading the* Evening Standard. OLIVE *is
lying on her bed. She is eating a marmalade
sandwich. The* NIGHT NURSE *comes in.*

NIGHT NURSE: Good evening, ladies. What's your name,
dear?

JANET: Janet.

NIGHT NURSE: Are you all right there?

50

JANET: Yes, thank you.

NIGHT NURSE: There's a television room outside. Or there is a little room along the corridor if you want to play some records. Only let me know if you want to use it because I have to keep it locked. The records have a habit of disappearing. You've got your locker and everything, have you, dear?

JANET: Yes, thanks.

NIGHT NURSE: Good. Oh well. I think I'll go and watch 'The Sweeney'.

[*The* NIGHT NURSE *goes off.* DENNIS *comes in from the other end of the dormitory. He is wearing his pyjamas and dressing-gown and is carrying a sponge bag. He has a towel slung over his shoulder.*]

DENNIS: [*to* JANET] Hello.

JANET: Hello.

DENNIS: Er . . . I'm sorry about earlier on.

JANET: That's all right.

DENNIS: I don't know what you must think. It was just such a shock being told to go like that. They're all very nice when you first come in but they gradually turn the other way. Oh. About the pictures. I mean, I'm not going for another week yet.

JANET: I might not be staying here myself.

DENNIS: Oh, I see. Oh well, forget it then.

JANET: I'm seriously thinking of leaving in the morning. I don't think I'm going to be able to stand it in here.

OLIVE: Get off into your own dormitory.

DENNIS: I'm just going. I wasn't asking you for a date or nothing like that. I was only trying to be sociable, that's all.

JANET: I know.

51

OLIVE: Do your dressing-gown up. We don't want to see everything you've got.

[DENNIS *adjusts his dressing-gown.*]

DENNIS: I just thought we might have had something in common.

[*There is a knock on the door.*]

JANET: Come in.

[KIERAN *comes in.*]

KIERAN: Oh, there you are. Beg your pardon. You were a long time. They were wondering if you'd gone down the plughole.

DENNIS: I'll be out in a minute.

KIERAN: D'you want a cup of Bournvita before all the milk disappears?

DENNIS: Yeah. I'll have one.

KIERAN: What about you, Janet?

JANET: Yes please.

KIERAN: Sorry to disturb you.

DENNIS: You wasn't disturbing no-one.

KIERAN: I'll go and get it.

DENNIS: You coming outside?

JANET: Yes.

[DENNIS *goes out.*]

OLIVE: He's a married man, you know.

JANET: Yes, I know.

SCENE ELEVEN

The lounge. TREVOR *is playing* 'I'd Like to Get You on a Slow Boat to China' *on his saxophone.* WALLY *is singing.* DENNIS *comes in and sits down.* KIERAN *comes in with five cups. He is singing as he comes in. He puts the cups down on the table.* JANET *comes out and sits down.* DENNIS *picks up his cup.*

DENNIS: What's this?

KIERAN: It's Bournvita. That's what you wanted, isn't it?

DENNIS: Yeah, but where's the Bournvita?

KIERAN: It's inside of the cup. Give it a stir.

DENNIS: There's no Bournvita in this cup, Kieran. There's nothing in here except milk.

WALLY: There's none in mine either. Have you got any, Janet?

JANET: It doesn't look like it.

KIERAN: Oh, sorry. Sorry. I must have forgotten to put it in. Give me the cups and I'll go and do it.

DENNIS: No, don't take the cups away. Bring the Bournvita in here.

KIERAN: Oh. Right.

[KIERAN *goes off.* DENNIS *gets out the communal carrier bag.*]

DENNIS: Anyone want a Jaffa Cake?

WALLY: Yes please.

TREVOR: I'll have one.

[KIERAN *comes back with an institution tin of Bournvita. The* NIGHT NURSE *comes in and rings a handbell.*]

WALLY: Tablet time. Only this time of the night you get your knock-out drops.

[*They all get up and go off.*]

SCENE TWELVE

The female dormitory. In the dark. OLIVE *is asleep on her back. She is snoring loudly.* JANET *is lying on top of the bed in her dressing-gown. The* NIGHT NURSE *comes in and shines a torch on* JANET.

NIGHT NURSE: Can't you get to sleep, dear?

JANET: No.

NIGHT NURSE: I expect it feels a bit strange. Mind you, that Valium should have made you feel sleepy.

JANET: They don't have any effect on me.

NIGHT NURSE: I'm surprised they haven't put you down for a sleeping pill. If you're not asleep in half an hour I'll give you another Valium. Only I wouldn't mention it to anybody else. Get into bed now and I'll tuck you in.

JANET: Oh, no, I couldn't.

NIGHT NURSE: Why not?

JANET: I can't get under the sheets.

NIGHT NURSE: Don't be silly. You'll catch your death like that.

JANET: I don't care. If I get under the sheets I'll start going hot and cold again and getting those horrible feelings in my stomach.

NIGHT NURSE: No you won't. Nothing's going to happen. I'm just outside if you need me. Come on.

JANET: No, I can't.

NIGHT NURSE: You don't mean to say you sleep on top of the bed at home.

JANET: No. I sleep in a chair at home.
 [*The door opens and* SYLVIA *comes staggering in. The* NIGHT NURSE *tuts.*]

NIGHT NURSE: Don't you make any noise. I don't know where you think you've been till this time. You'd have been better off staying out for the night.

SYLVIA: Can I have my Mogadon?

NIGHT NURSE: No you can't. You've had too much to drink.

SYLVIA: Oh, go on, nurse. Let me have one. Go on. Please. It won't hurt.

NIGHT NURSE: Oh, well, on your own head be it. You can come out and get it. And then get into bed as

quick as you can. Before you wake up everybody else.

SYLVIA: I don't know how they can sleep through all
that snoring.

NIGHT NURSE: Come and help me turn her over.

> [*They go over to* OLIVE's *bed, pull
> back the covers and turn her on to
> her side.*]

God, she weighs a ton. There. That ought
to shut you up, my girl.

SCENE THIRTEEN

The lounge. DENNIS, WALLY *and* KIERAN
are sitting on the couch. TREVOR *is walking
up and down angrily with a bottle of milk.*
JANET *comes in with four cups of tea.*
DENNIS *gets out the communal carrier bag.*

WALLY: We'd better show our faces in Pottery this
morning.

DENNIS: It's hardly worth my while, seeing as how
I'm not going to be here.

WALLY: Oh, come on, we'll have a laugh.

DENNIS: I don't feel like laughing.

WALLY: [*to* KIERAN] Are you going to O.T. this
morning?

KIERAN: I think I will. I have to finish off me master-
piece.

WALLY: He does lovely paintings, Kieran does,
don't you.

KIERAN: I do not. I'm no good at all.

WALLY: Well, I think they're very good.

> [SYLVIA *comes out of the dormitory
> in her dressing-gown, with a cup in
> her hand. She goes off to the
> kitchen.*]

DENNIS: She looks as if she's had a night of it.

KIERAN: Out on the tiles again last night, I suppose.

WALLY: I bet he don't know nothing about it. The one who comes in here and does all her washing.

JANET: Oh, I thought that was her husband.

KIERAN: Not at all. She's only dangling him on a string.

WALLY: You know she's got two black daughters.

JANET: She did say she had some children. But I didn't realise they were coloured.

DENNIS: Only the daughters are coloured. They've been in here a couple of times. They're living with their father by all accounts.

WALLY: The little boy's white, though, isn't he?

DENNIS: Yeah. I don't think it's his, though. The one who comes in here.

JANET: She seems like quite a nice person, though.

WALLY: She might be if you got to know her. Never talks to us. Not a bit friendly like yourself.

DENNIS: I'd have more respect for her if she acted like a woman of her age.

KIERAN: She'd be better if she put on a nice frock. Or trousers that'd fit without the two cheeks wobbling.

WALLY: Yeah, you're right. Oh well. I think we'd better be going down to Pottery.

DENNIS: I'm not going. Sod 'em.

WALLY: Oh, go on, Dennis.

DENNIS: No.

WALLY: Oh, all right then. You coming, Kieran?

KIERAN: Yeah.

> [KIERAN *and* WALLY *go off.* JANET *gets up.*]

JANET: D'you want another cup of tea, Dennis?

DENNIS: No. Not just now, thanks. Er . . . Do you like Charles Bronson at all?

JANET: Yes, he's all right.

DENNIS: He's on at the ABC.

JANET: Is he?

> [SYLVIA *comes out of the kitchen.*]

Did you have a good time last night?

> [SYLVIA *comes over.*]

SYLVIA: Oh yes, thanks. But I've got a terrible headache this morning.

> [SYLVIA *sits down.* DENNIS *gets up and goes off.*]

SYLVIA: Old misery-guts.

JANET: He keeps asking me to go out with him.

SYLVIA: What, to the pictures?

JANET: Yes.

SYLVIA: He kept asking me to go when I first came in. I told him to piss off. That's why he doesn't speak to me.

> [VICKY *comes up to* JANET *with a piece of paper in her hand.*]

VICKY: How are you this morning, Janet?

JANET: All right.

VICKY: Good. Could we have a word about occupational therapy?

JANET: Yes.

> [VICKY *sits down.*]

VICKY: What do you like to do in your spare time?

JANET: Nothing special. I stay in and read or I go out and visit my friends.

VICKY: Are you interested in any of the arts and crafts?

JANET: Not really. I'm not very good with my hands. It's not compulsory this, is it?

VICKY: No, it's not. But do have a look at the list. You might see something that catches your eye.

> [JANET *looks at the list.*]

SYLVIA: Vicky, could I have a couple of aspirin,

	please? I've got a headache.
VICKY:	Yes. I'll get them for you in a minute.
JANET:	Oh. You've got typing.
VICKY:	Oh yes.
JANET:	I can type but I don't use all the right fingers. I've always said I'd learn to type properly one day.
VICKY:	If you're interested I could take you down to the class this afternoon.
JANET:	I haven't quite decided yet. I have got a good speed as it is. It might not be worth my while learning again after such a long time.
VICKY:	I'll get you the aspirin, Sylvia.

[VICKY *goes off.*]

| JANET: | What O.T. do you do? |
| SYLVIA: | I don't. Bugger all that. I've come in here to have a holiday. |

[TREVOR *comes up to* SYLVIA.]

TREVOR:	Will you be going to the pub again tonight?
SYLVIA:	Eh?
TREVOR:	Will you be going to the pub?
SYLVIA:	What?

[SYLVIA *looks at* JANET.]

What's he saying?

[JANET *shakes her head.*]

| TREVOR: | I don't want to shout in case anybody hears. |

[SYLVIA *looks at him blankly.* DR WILSON *comes in.*]

Oh, sod the lot of you.

[TREVOR *goes off and kicks the furniture.*]

| DR WILSON: | Shall I see you now, Janet? |
| JANET: | Oh. Yes. |

[JANET *gets up and goes off with* DR WILSON. VICKY *comes in with a cup of water and two aspirins, which she gives to* SYLVIA.]

SCENE FOURTEEN
The psychiatrist's office. DR WILSON *and*
JANET *are facing each other.*

JANET: I wanted to ask you if I could have my other
tablets back. My doctor told me I shouldn't
stop taking them suddenly.

DR WILSON: We're giving you Valium instead, so you
needn't feel anxious about any possible side
effects. Have you had any funny feelings
since you came into hospital?

JANET: No. But I've taken a lot more Valium than
you prescribed for me. I got them from
another patient. She keeps them in her
handbag. [*Pause.*] The woman in the next
bed to me. And the night nurse thought I
should have a sleeping pill.

DR WILSON: It's quite unnecessary, Janet. We don't
think you need to be taking any drugs
at all.

JANET: I didn't ask for them in the first place, did I.
I was given them by my doctor because I had
to keep going to him with illnesses that he
said was nerves. But I'm only nervous
because I feel as if there's something wrong
with me physically. Will I be having any
tests while I'm in here?

DR WILSON: What sort of tests?

JANET: Well... I know there's a machine for testing
the brain.

DR WILSON: We're not going to do anything like that.

JANET: But how else can you tell if somebody's got
something wrong inside their head? I mean
... Like ... Well, like a tumour.

DR WILSON: As far as I can tell, Janet, you're in good
physical health.

JANET: Oh. So you think it's mental, whatever's

wrong with me. I'm not like all those
others out there, though, am I? You can see
they're all, well, a bit peculiar in one way
or another. How long have I got to be in
here?

DR WILSON: We'll see how you get on, shall we? I'll see
you again in a few days.

SCENE FIFTEEN
The female dormitory. SYLVIA *is sitting on
her bed. She is putting a white face-pack on
her face.* OLIVE *is not there. But from the
bathroom comes the sound of her loudly
intoning a pagan song from the old
religion.* JANET *comes in.*

JANET: What's that noise?

SYLVIA: It's Olive having a bath. You get this every
morning. A waste of time if you ask me. She
only puts the same old clothes back on
again afterwards.

JANET: Ugh.

SYLVIA: You never see her do any washing. I
wouldn't have much to do with her if I were
you.

[DR WILSON *comes in and goes up to*
SYLVIA.]

DR WILSON: Shall I see you now, Sylvia?

SYLVIA: Yes, all right. But you'll have to excuse the
face.

[SYLVIA *goes off with* DR WILSON.
OLIVE *comes out of the bathroom.*]

SCENE SIXTEEN
The psychiatrist's office. DR WILSON *and*
SYLVIA *are facing each other.* SYLVIA *takes a
piece of paper out of her handbag.*

SYLVIA: I've filled out the form for the Council. But I need you to write a letter to them as well. They get millions of transfer applications. The only chance you have of getting one is on the grounds of ill health.

DR WILSON: I'm afraid we've found in the past that letters from us are not given any special consideration.

SYLVIA: Can't you write them a really good letter? See where it says 'Areas Preferred'. Well, I don't want to live in a council flat that looks like a council flat so I've put down Knightsbridge, Kensington and Chelsea. I know they've got some flats and houses tucked away round there only they keep it very quiet. You're not supposed to know. You can tell them I'm not on Social Security. Not like everybody else on my estate. You can't get a look in at the local post office for them all cashing in their Giro cheques. Are you going to write a letter for me?

DR WILSON: Even if you do get a transfer, Sylvia, it's not going to happen overnight. I think you'll have to be prepared to make the best of where you are for the time being.

SYLVIA: It's all right for you to sit there and tell me what to make the best of. You don't come out of your front door and step on a pile of dogshit. And I bet your neighbours don't leave parcels of curry and rice on the stairs.

DR WILSON: I used to live in Peckham.

SYLVIA: You what?

DR WILSON: I'll see you again in a few days, Sylvia.

[SYLVIA *rubs some of the face-pack off her face.*]

SYLVIA: It's a pity the wrinkles don't come off with it.

61

SCENE SEVENTEEN

The female dormitory. OLIVE *is lying on her bed. She is eating some chocolates out of a crumpled paper bag.* JANET *comes in, flings herself on to her bed and sobs.*

OLIVE: D'you want a chocolate, dear?

JANET: No.

OLIVE: Yes you do.

JANET: I don't. I don't eat sweets. They're bad for your teeth.

> [OLIVE *comes over to* JANET *and puts a chocolate into* JANET'*s mouth.*]

OLIVE: These ones are good for you, dear. They're home-made. My friend sends them over from the Continent. Who's been upsetting you, dear?

JANET: The woman in the typing class. A right old bitch. She sat me down and showed me some typing exercises. I lit up a cigarette and she said: 'Put that out. You can't type and smoke.' So I said I have been typing and smoking for fourteen years. 'You won't in here,' she said, so I got up and walked out.

OLIVE: You're like me, dear. Over-sensitive. I never could take anyone telling me off. I was always crying when I was a young girl. I don't cry any more, though. I've run out of tears. I used to feel sorry for other people as well. Even if I didn't know them I'd feel for them. I felt ever so sorry for poor Al Capone. Well, I knew what was going to happen, you see. It was all in the cards. I did write and tell him but I don't think he could have got my letter in time. Would you like me to read the cards for you, dear?

JANET: Oh no. I'd be too scared.

OLIVE: I wouldn't tell you anything bad, dear.

JANET: Can you really tell what's going to happen?

OLIVE: Oh yes, dear.

> [OLIVE *takes a pack of cards out of her pocket.*]

Shuffle the cards and cut them into three, dear. Now put them all together again in a pile and pick out seven cards from anywhere you like. Now lay them on the bed, face down.

> [JANET *shuffles and picks out the cards.*]

OLIVE: You've picked out quite a few spades, dear. There's been a lot of disappointment in your life. And a lot of worries. But there's money in the bank and your health is better than average.

JANET: Are you sure?

OLIVE: The cards never lie. You'll be getting a letter from a fair-haired lady. She's offering you a sum of money. You'll be taking up new employment. Not for some time but when the frost is underfoot. You've got a lot of gentlemen here, dear. But they're all surrounded by trouble and indecision. You've had a lot of bad luck with men, haven't you, dear? Like me. Only I was always attracted to perverts. Who's this man here? He's from another town. Manchester.

JANET: I did go out with somebody from Birmingham.

OLIVE: That's what I meant. You'll be seeing him again.

JANET: I was thinking of ringing him up.

OLIVE: Oh no, you mustn't ring men up, dear. When you want to see him again you go

63

down to the shops first and buy a big red
candle. Take a needle and stick it into the
candle. Then light it up and wait. When the
needle falls out of the candle, he'll be in
touch. That'll be £1.50, dear.

JANET: Oh.

OLIVE: You can give it to me later.

[OLIVE *picks up a perfume spray.*]
Have some of this. It'll make you smell nice.

[OLIVE *sprays perfume all over*
JANET.]

SCENE EIGHTEEN

The lounge. Early evening. TREVOR *is
playing* 'South of the Border Down Mexico
Way' *on his saxophone.* JANET, SYLVIA *and*
KIERAN *are sitting on the couch.* KIERAN *is
singing. On the floor is a heap of suitcases
and MacMarket carrier bags with the
contents spilling out on to the floor. The*
NIGHT NURSE *comes in.*

NIGHT NURSE: Good evening, ladies. Good evening,
gentlemen. Now what's all this doing on
the floor?

JANET: It's Dennis's luggage, nurse. He hasn't
quite finished his packing yet.

NIGHT NURSE: He's got no business leaving it till this time
of night. He should have been out of here by
this morning.

KIERAN: He was waiting for some of his washing to
dry.

[*The* NIGHT NURSE *stacks the
luggage into a pile.*]

NIGHT NURSE: Huh. A fine way to pack.

[WALLY *comes out of the male
dormitory.*]

WALLY: Nurse. He's locked himself in the lavatory.

NIGHT NURSE: Who has?

WALLY: Dennis. I've been banging on the door but he won't answer.

NIGHT NURSE: All right. Thank you, Wally. You go and sit down and leave it to me.

> [*The* NIGHT NURSE *goes off.* WALLY *sits down.*]

WALLY: [*to* JANET] You can't actually lock yourself in. They've got a special key. Just in case anyone tries something silly.

SCENE NINETEEN
The lavatory. DENNIS *is sitting on the seat with a paper cup of water and a large bottle of aspirins from Boots The Chemist. The* NIGHT NURSE *has opened the door.*

NIGHT NURSE: I'll have those, thank you very much. How many have you taken?

> [DENNIS *doesn't answer.*]

I said how many have you taken?

DENNIS: I haven't taken any yet.

NIGHT NURSE: Good. Now get up off there and go and wash your hands and face. And smarten yourself up. You look a sight.

DENNIS: I've got a lot more tablets at home.

NIGHT NURSE: Well, you'd better go home and kill yourself. I'll ring up for a taxi.

> [DENNIS *starts kicking the walls. The* NIGHT NURSE *tries to stop him but* DENNIS *struggles with her.*]

All right, Dennis. Have it your own way. I won't call for a taxi. I'll send for a policeman instead.

> [*She goes off.*]

SCENE TWENTY
The lounge. The NIGHT NURSE *comes in.*

NIGHT NURSE: I've sent for a policeman. That ought to bring him to his senses.

WALLY: Shall I take some of his luggage out to the front?

NIGHT NURSE: No, you stop where you are, my lad.

[*She goes off.* TREVOR *starts to play* 'I'm Looking Over a Four-Leaf Clover.']

JANET: We used to do that one at my dancing class.

SYLVIA: Did you go to tap and ballet?

JANET: Yes.

SYLVIA: So did I.

[SYLVIA *does a time step, sitting down.* JANET *does a double time step, sitting down.*]

KIERAN: Good girl. That's just like the Irish step dance.

[SYLVIA *and* JANET *get up and do a triple time step.* KIERAN *gets up and does an Irish dance.* TREVOR *changes the tune to an Irish jig.* KIERAN *dances on his own and the others clap their hands.*]

END OF ACT ONE

ACT TWO

SCENE ONE

The female dormitory. JANET *and* SYLVIA *are tap-dancing to music from the record player: a thirties record of* 'Isn't it a Lovely Day'. *They are both wearing tap shoes.* JANET *is wearing a leotard and* SYLVIA *is wearing cut-down denims.* CYRIL *comes in. They stop dancing.* SYLVIA *stops the music.*

SYLVIA: What d'you want?

CYRIL: I just want to say, if you went over to the gymnasium you'd have a lot more room. I could carry the record player over for you.

SYLVIA: I don't want to go over there, do you, Janet?

JANET: No.

SYLVIA: We don't want people staring at us.

CYRIL: All right, then. Carry on dancing.

[CYRIL *sits down.*]

SYLVIA: Not in front of you.

JANET: You're making me feel embarrassed.

SYLVIA: He only wants to look at our legs.

CYRIL: Huh. I do not.

SYLVIA: Well, leave us alone, then. We're not doing anything wrong, are we?

CYRIL: Of course not.

SYLVIA: You're always saying I should be doing O.T. Well, now I am, aren't I. This is our own O.T. And we don't need any supervision. Is that all right?

[CYRIL *gets up and goes out.*]

Nosey sod.

JANET: I bet that Vicky told him to keep an eye on us.

SYLVIA: Yeah. It worries the life out of them if you try to do anything out of the ordinary.

> [SYLVIA *starts the record up again and they do a few more steps.*]

SYLVIA: Cor blimey. I'm really puffed out.

JANET: We'll have to stop smoking, you know.

SYLVIA: Yeah. I'm going to really start cutting down from tomorrow.

JANET: So am I, for definite. D'you want one?

SYLVIA: Yeah.

> [*They light up cigarettes.*]

SCENE TWO

The lounge. WALLY *and* KIERAN *are sitting on the couch.* VICKY *comes in with* GEORGE *who is carrying a very heavy rucksack on his back. They go off towards the male dormitory.*

KIERAN: Is he coming in here on his holidays, or what?

WALLY: I hope he's not going to pitch a tent up in there.

> [CYRIL *comes in and goes up to* WALLY.]

CYRIL: Would you come with me now, please, Wally? And you too, Kieran.

> [KIERAN *and* WALLY *get up and go off with* CYRIL.]

SCENE THREE

The female dormitory. OLIVE *is lying on her bed.* JANET *and* SYLVIA *are getting changed.*

SYLVIA: Cor, my muscles are really aching.

JANET: So are mine. We must be doing ourselves some good. I've got ever so flabby since I came in here.

SYLVIA: I was flabby before I came in. If I had the money I'd go to one of those clinics where you can lie on your back and let them pummel off the inches.

JANET: I'd go and have all my silver fillings taken out and get them to do white ones instead.

SYLVIA: They can take all the hair off your legs and that and it never grows back again.

JANET: I wonder what they can do about your nails. I read in a magazine that if you took three tablespoons of gelatine a day it'd make your nails go strong. I tried it but it only worked on my toenails. They've gone rock hard. But my fingernails are still like paper.

SYLVIA: Ask Dr Wilson. I'm going to ask him about my wart. If you want anything special seeing to while you're in here you stand a better chance of getting it done. For psychological reasons.

JANET: I've always wanted somebody to have a look at my belly button. It's not the same as other people's.

SYLVIA: It looks all right to me.

JANET: No, it's not. It juts out more on one side than the other. I've never yet got up the nerve to mention it to a doctor. They think you're being fussy about nothing.

SYLVIA: It's the same with my wart, really. I keep meaning to tell Dr Wilson only I'm scared he might want to have a look at it. I wouldn't want him to see it. I only want him to send me to a specialist. It's in a funny place. You know. I think it's a wart. Or it might be a mole.

OLIVE: You mustn't let anyone ever touch a mole. I knew a man who had a mole cut off his back. Four days later he collapsed. He was dead by the time they got him to hospital.

SYLVIA: Oh, leave off, will you! You can't have a conversation in here.

OLIVE: It was on his left side, poor man. A mole on the left is always a sign of danger.

SYLVIA: It's lucky mine's on the right, then, isn't it.

OLIVE: Ah, but whereabouts is it?

SYLVIA: I'll give you three guesses.

OLIVE: I wouldn't want to guess. All I know is that a mole on the private parts is the sign of a hypocrite.

SYLVIA: Oh, thanks very much.

JANET: I've got a big mole on my neck. I wonder what that's supposed to mean.

OLIVE: A mole upon the neck is the sign of wealth and fame, dear.

JANET: Oh good. That's all right then.

OLIVE: Unless it's on the nape of the neck.

JANET: Oh no.

OLIVE: According to the seers of ancient times all those with a mole upon the nape of the neck will be beheaded.

SYLVIA: Oh, don't be so daft.

JANET: That can't be true, can it?

OLIVE: You might be able to avert it, dear, but the threat is always there. Look at me. I'm cursed with a mole upon the throat. The sign of a glutton. There's a voice inside me all the time, nagging at me to eat. If I don't fill myself up enough during the day I'm persecuted by night with dreams of bakeries and Italian ice-cream parlours.

SYLVIA: Oh, go and have a marmalade sandwich. And I hope it chokes you.

JANET: I bet I'll be dreaming about guillotines tonight.

SCENE FOUR

The lounge. TREVOR *is walking up and down with a bottle of milk.* MRS O'TOOLE *comes striding in.*

TREVOR: Kieran's gone to have his treatment.

MRS O'TOOLE: What?

TREVOR: He's gone for his treatment.

[MRS O'TOOLE *smiles and nods at him but without understanding.* SYLVIA *and* JANET *come out of the female dormitory.* JANET *goes up to* MRS O'TOOLE.]

JANET: Oh, Mrs O'Toole. I think Kieran must have gone to have his treatment. Would you like a cup of tea?

MRS O'TOOLE: Thank you very much, dear. That's very nice of you.

[JANET *goes off.* SYLVIA *and* MRS O'TOOLE *sit down.* MRS O'TOOLE *gets out her knitting.*]

That girl is looking a lot worse since ever she came in here. I don't think she should be in here at all.

SYLVIA: I shouldn't think she'll be here for very long.

MRS O'TOOLE: There's nothing much the matter with her.

SYLVIA: She is very nervous, though, you know.

MRS O'TOOLE: Ah, she's no more nervous than anybody else. If they brought everybody who was nervous into here the streets would be deserted.

> [VICKY *comes in with* GEORGE, *who is carrying a copy of* 'Saturn — A New Look at an Old Devil'.]

VICKY: Oh, George, I'd like you to meet Sylvia.

SYLVIA: Hi.

GEORGE: Hello.

MRS O'TOOLE: Hello, George. I'm Mrs O'Toole. My husband is a patient on this ward.

GEORGE: Hello.

VICKY: Would you like to sit down, George?

GEORGE: Thank you.

> [VICKY *goes off.* GEORGE *goes and sits down over the other side. He opens his book and takes out a packet of Gauloises.* JANET *comes in with the tea and gets the sugar out of the communal carrier bag under the couch.*]

SYLVIA: George.

GEORGE: Yes?

SYLVIA: D'you fancy a cup of tea?

GEORGE: Oh, yes please.

SYLVIA: You can have this if you like. I'll go and get myself another one. D'you take sugar?

GEORGE: Oh, yes please. Two and a half.

> [SYLVIA *gives her tea to* GEORGE *and goes off.*]

MRS O'TOOLE: [*whispering*] She couldn't give it to him quick enough. Anything in a trousers. I like the way she puts on all the airs and graces. But she couldn't fool me for a minute, that one. I know where she lives.

JANET: Where?

MRS O'TOOLE: She has a flat on a rotten old estate. You know the kind I mean; like an old army barracks. Where they shove in all the dregs of society. I've walked past that estate a few

times and I seen a big black face hanging
over every balcony. Don't tell her I told you.
She doesn't like anyone to know she has a
council flat.

[SYLVIA *comes back with her tea.*]

SYLVIA: Would you like a biscuit, George?

GEORGE: Oh, yes please. Thank you very much.

[SYLVIA *takes some biscuits over to*
GEORGE. CYRIL *comes in with*
KIERAN *and* WALLY.]

MRS O'TOOLE: Oh, God help the two of them. Hello, Cyril.

CYRIL: Hello, Mrs O'Toole. He'll be all right again
in a little while.

[CYRIL *goes off.* WALLY *and* KIERAN
sit down. They look a bit dazed.]

MRS O'TOOLE: Do you want any tea, the pair of yous?

WALLY: No.

KIERAN: I could drink a Guinness.

[MRS O'TOOLE *gets out a packet of*
sweets.]

MRS O'TOOLE: You can have a Spangle.

[*She offers them around.*]

D'you want a Spangle, George?

GEORGE: Yes please.

MRS O'TOOLE: Come over here and get it.

[GEORGE *comes over.*]

What's that you're reading?

GEORGE: It's about astrology.

MRS O'TOOLE: Oh, that's very interesting. I read me stars
every day in the *Express* and they often
come true.

GEORGE: It's not that kind of astrology.

MRS O'TOOLE: Isn't it? I didn't know there was any other
kind.

GEORGE: Oh yes. This is serious astrology.

[KIERAN *picks up* SYLVIA's *tea and*
has a sip.]

73

MRS O'TOOLE: Put that down. That's Sylvia's tea.

KIERAN: Oh, I'm sorry. I beg your pardon, Janet.

MRS O'TOOLE: [*to* SYLVIA] I'm sorry about that. [*to* KIERAN] You said you didn't want any.

> [GEORGE *turns round and starts walking back to his place.*]

What sign d'you think I am, George?

GEORGE: I wouldn't like to say.

MRS O'TOOLE: I'm a typical Gemini. What are you?

> [GEORGE *comes back again.*]

GEORGE: I'm a Pisces. But there's a lot more to it than that.

SYLVIA: I'm a Leo.

WALLY: Oh, the same as my mother. I'm a whatsname myself. Taurus. What are you, Kieran?

KIERAN: I don't know. [*to* MRS O'TOOLE] What am I?

MRS O'TOOLE: You're a Capricorn the goat.

JANET: I'm not sure what I am. Some of them say I'm a Cancer but other ones say I'm a Gemini.

MRS O'TOOLE: This is Janet, by the way, George.

JANET: Hello.

GEORGE: Hello, Janet. It sounds as if you're on the cusp. But in actual fact you must be one sign or the other. The only way you could find out for sure is if you knew the actual time you were born.

JANET: I do know the time I was born. It was twenty past four in the morning.

GEORGE: Are you absolutely a hundred percent certain?

JANET: Yes.

GEORGE: There's not a lot of people who can tell you their true time of birth. It wouldn't be on your birth certificate unless you're a twin or you happen to come from Scotland.

74

JANET: My Mum had a little card that they put on my cot in the nursing home. It tells you the time I was born and the circumference of my head.

GEORGE: That's wonderful. When's your birthday?

JANET: The 21st of June.

GEORGE: What year?

JANET: Nineteen forty . . . d'you have to have the year?

GEORGE: I don't have to. But I was going to say I could do you a chart if you like.

JANET: You mean a proper horoscope? I've always wanted to have one of those done.

GEORGE: It could tell you quite a lot about the sort of person you are.

MRS O'TOOLE: Go on and tell him the year and we'll put our hands up over our ears. I don't know what you have to worry about. You're only a young girl.

JANET: No I'm not, you know. I'll give it him later.

MRS O'TOOLE: I'd like to know the sort of person I am. But I couldn't tell you the time I was born. It was too long ago. Are you married, George?

GEORGE: Oh no.

KIERAN: Don't be asking questions.

MRS O'TOOLE: He doesn't mind, do you, George? Have you got a girl-friend?

GEORGE: Yes. I've got a few.

KIERAN: Good luck to you. If I was on me own I'd find myself a couple of fancy women.

MRS O'TOOLE: Well, you needn't think I'm going to stop you. What I'd like to do is to have an affair.

KIERAN: Oh, would you.

MRS O'TOOLE: I would. [*to* SYLVIA] I wonder how would you go about having one?

KIERAN: Will you be quiet.

WALLY: I wouldn't mind having an affair myself.

75

Perhaps you and me could have an affair together, Mrs O'Toole.

MRS O'TOOLE: If I had an affair with anybody in here, it'd be Cyril. He's a lovely fellow, God bless him. It's a pity he wasn't white. Not that I have anything at all against the blacks. I suppose you must soon get used to them. Where was it your husband was from, Sylvia?

SYLVIA: He was a British subject. Which is more than what you are.

MRS O'TOOLE: You don't know what you're talking about. I am a British subject, aren't I, Kieran?

KIERAN: Not at all.

MRS O'TOOLE: I am.

KIERAN: You are not.

MRS O'TOOLE: You might not think you are but I know I am.

SYLVIA: You don't come from the North of Ireland, do you?

MRS O'TOOLE: I do not. I come from the South.

KIERAN: Up the rebels.

MRS O'TOOLE: Never mind the rebels. I've lived in this country for nearly thirty years. And Kieran was over here in the army during the war.

KIERAN: God save the Queen.

MRS O'TOOLE: Oh, shut up. You won't be serious, that's the trouble with you. You couldn't be serious if it was to save your life.

[CYRIL *comes in and rings a hand-bell.*]

WALLY: Tablet time. [*to* GEORGE] We have to go and queue up at the counter.

GEORGE: Oh. Should I come with you?

WALLY: You better ask Cyril.

[GEORGE *goes up to* CYRIL.]

GEORGE: Do I have to go and queue up?

76

CYRIL: Yes, that's right. You follow the others.
> [WALLY, KIERAN, JANET, SYLVIA
> *and* GEORGE *go off.*]

MRS O'TOOLE: How are you today, Cyril?

CYRIL: I'm fine, thanks, Mrs O'Toole. How is the indigestion?

MRS O'TOOLE: It's a lot better, thank you, Cyril. But I'm still feeling depressed. And I'm exhausted from the journey up here every day. When I get home at night there isn't a bit of life left in me.

CYRIL: Why don't you stay at home, Mrs O'Toole, and take it easy for a couple of days?

MRS O'TOOLE: Oh, I couldn't. He'd only worry if I didn't come in and see him. I don't want him to realise how depressed I am. But how am I going to hide it? I think I need to be taking some of them Valium.

SCENE FIVE

The female dormitory. Early evening.
OLIVE *is lying on her bed. She is shuffling a pack of cards.* JANET *is lying on her bed.* SYLVIA *is painting her toenails. There is a knock at the door.*

SYLVIA: Come in.
> [BRIAN *comes in with some bags.*
> *He is smartly dressed.*]

BRIAN: Hello, luv.

SYLVIA: Oh. What are you doing here?

BRIAN: I thought I'd come up tonight instead of coming in tomorrow dinnertime.

SYLVIA: Who's looking after Benjamin?

BRIAN: I've left him with them next door.

SYLVIA: You could have rung up and told me.

BRIAN: I didn't think you'd mind, luv. I thought if

you wanted to we could go out somewhere
nice and have a meal.

SYLVIA: I'm already going out.

BRIAN: Oh, I see. Where are you going to?

SYLVIA: It's none of your business.

BRIAN: Oh, all right, luv. I didn't mean to upset
you. I've washed your black dress for you.
It's come up very nice. And there's a box of
Maltesers and a couple of toilet rolls. Oh,
and I got you some tights. I didn't get them
from t'market. There were a bloke selling
them off at work. Three pair for 35p.

SYLVIA: They're the wrong sort.

BRIAN: I can't see anything wrong with them. All
t'fellows were buying them up at work for
their wives.

SYLVIA: Well, I'm not wearing tights with re-
inforcements at the top. They come half-
way down your flipping leg. Don't keep
bringing me in things I don't want.

BRIAN: All right, I'm sorry. I won't ever bring you
in anything again. Unless you tell me to.
Are you going out with Janet?

SYLVIA: No, I'm not.

BRIAN: Oh, I see.

[*He sits down on* SYLVIA's *bed.*]

You're looking very nice tonight, luv.

SYLVIA: You needn't park yourself down there
because I'm going.

[SYLVIA *puts on her socks and
boots.*]

BRIAN: Couldn't we go outside and have a little
talk?

SYLVIA: No. I haven't got time.

BRIAN: I only mean for a minute.

SYLVIA: No.

BRIAN: Just for a couple of seconds, Sylvia, please.

SYLVIA: I said no. Look, Brian, just piss off out of it, will you?

OLIVE: You mind that language.

SYLVIA: And you can piss off and all. I'm fed up to the teeth with her fucking interfering and I'm fed up with you flapping around after me all the time.

OLIVE: Huh.

[SYLVIA *throws some things into her locker and slings some make-up into her handbag.*]

BRIAN: There's no need to get yourself into a state, now, luv.

SYLVIA: I'm not in a state. Look, just pick up your tights and go.

BRIAN: I am going. I just wanted to say . . .
[*He puts his arm round her.*]

SYLVIA: Get off. Take your hands off me. Get off or I'll call the nurse. I don't want you to touch me. And I don't want to see you in here ever again.
[*She goes off.*]

BRIAN: [*to* JANET] She doesn't mean it. We've had these little tiffs before. I don't know what started it off, though. What did I say to upset her?

JANET: I don't know.

BRIAN: Did she say where she was going to, Janet? I know she confides in you.

JANET: No, she didn't say.

BRIAN: She'll probably tell me herself. She usually does tell me everything. She's told me all about her past life, you know. She's going out with a feller, isn't she?

JANET: It's not for me to say. I don't want to get into any trouble.

BRIAN: How did she meet him? He can't be up to

79

any good if he's taking out a psychiatric patient.

JANET: I think it's somebody she's known for a long time.

BRIAN: Oh. So you think it might just be platonic, like.

JANET: It probably is. She did say he was quite happily married.

BRIAN: Oh. Did she say owt else?

JANET: She said he's got a green Toyota.

BRIAN: Oh, has he. You don't think it's anything serious, though, do you?

JANET: No, I don't suppose so.

[BRIAN *sits down on* JANET's *bed.*]

OLIVE: You shouldn't be in here, you know.

[BRIAN *stands up.*]

BRIAN: She takes a lot of understanding, does Sylvia. She's very highly strung, you see. She's got a mind of her own but she wants looking after at t'same time. She's right intelligent, too, you know. And she's such a fantastic looking girl, isn't she, eh? I'd do anything in the world for her, I would you know. I don't mind telling you, Janet, I worship t'bloody ground she walks on. When she gets back tonight you can tell her I'm sorry for upsetting her. I keep on forgetting she's not well. If these tights are any good to you, Janet, you're quite welcome to have them.

JANET: Well . . . I don't know really.

OLIVE: I'd have them only I haven't gone over to tights yet. I'm still in stockings.

[OLIVE *lifts up her dress to show her stockings. A handbell rings outside. The* NIGHT NURSE *comes in.*]

NIGHT NURSE: All visitors out. [*to* BRIAN] You shouldn't be in here, you know.

OLIVE: That's just what I said to him.

SCENE SIX

The lounge. WALLY *and* KIERAN *are sitting on chairs.* WALLY *has his eyes closed.* KIERAN *is watching* GEORGE, *who is sitting on the couch with a blank astrological chart, an ephemeris, several books on astrology, pens, paper, and a cup of tea in front of him on the table.* DR WILSON *comes in and goes up to* GEORGE.

DR WILSON: Shall I see you now, George?

GEORGE: Oh no. It's not convenient at the moment. I'm doing a chart. Could you give me another twenty minutes?

DR WILSON: No, I'm afraid I shall have to see you now, George.

GEORGE: I haven't got anything to say to you, really.

DR WILSON: I won't keep you for long.

GEORGE: Well, let me put Pluto in then I can leave it. There. [*He gets up.*] Oh no. I can't leave it here like this. Somebody might touch it.

DR WILSON: I'll be in my office.

[DR WILSON *goes off.* GEORGE *collects up all his things, including the cup of tea, and goes off.*]

KIERAN: Are you sleeping, Wally?

WALLY: No. No, I'm just resting my eyes.

KIERAN: I'm going to have a shower. I haven't had one since yesterday.

[KIERAN *strips down to his underwear, rolls up his clothes and runs off with the clothes under his arm.*]

SCENE SEVEN

The psychiatrist's office. DR WILSON *and* GEORGE *are facing each other.*

DR WILSON: How are you feeling, George?

GEORGE: I'm going through a very difficult time. I don't know if you know but Saturn has moved into Virgo. That's my opposite sign. What sign are you?

DR WILSON: I beg your pardon?

GEORGE: What astrological sign were you born under?

DR WILSON: I'm afraid I don't believe in any of that, George. My wife does, though.

[DR WILSON *smiles.* GEORGE *does not.*]

GEORGE: When were you born?

DR WILSON: Er . . . well, actually I was born in March.

GEORGE: What date?

DR WILSON: The twentieth.

GEORGE: Oh, amazing, the day after me. Pisces. You're probably going through the same kind of thing. Michaelangelo was a Pisces. So was Einstein. You'll find relationships with older people a bit of a hassle for the next couple of years. I've got Gemini on the ascendant and it's already started to affect my fourth house. There's been a lot of aggravation on the domestic front and it's gonna get worse. I don't know how I'm gonna handle it. Saturn's gonna be staying in Virgo for two and a half years. I need to be left alone to do what I'm trying to do. I'm trying to get a book together. I know I've got the talent and it should be a success because I've got the Sun in the tenth house

82

in conjunction with Venus, in Pisces, and Aquarius is on the mid-heaven. Mercury's in Pisces as well only it falls in the ninth house of higher communication. Mercury's my ruling planet. The trouble is, though, Venus is square Mercury and the Moon in my seventh house, in Sagittarius. So there's a conflict going on all the time. And unfortunately I've got the Sun and Venus in opposition to Neptune, which tends to make me feel disillusioned with my own creativity. Whenever that happens I have to lie down on the floor for the rest of the day and sometimes half the night and I can't do fuck all else until I can get it sorted out in my head.

DR WILSON: You've been feeling depressed, have you, lately?

GEORGE: Oh, Christ, no. I don't feel depressed. In fact I feel elated a lot of the time. That's why I can't go to work. I have to walk through the park to get to the station. It's such an amazing park. They've got roses all over the place and little wild flowers. And weeping willows leaning over the pond. There's a load of ducks and there's little squirrels hiding up in the trees. The conkers should be ready to fall at any moment now. I have to stop and look at it all and I think oh, fuck, it's all too much. And I have to turn back and go home. I get this feeling as if my heart is gonna come bursting out of my chest. How many beats should there be to the minute?

DR WILSON: It does tend to vary from person to person.

GEORGE: Yes, but just give me an idea of the average.

DR WILSON: Seventy-two is about normal.

GEORGE: Well, that's it then, isn't it. Mine's going too fast. I'm clocking up ninety-five and a hundred. I find myself having to keep checking it all the time. When I get back from the park I have to ring up the office and tell them I've got a case of dermatitis. Or a toothache. Then I can spend the day listening to Verdi and Puccini. I can't believe Puccini was a Capricorn. There's a lot of composers I haven't got round to yet. There's never enough time when I'm stuck in that office all day writing out invoice after fucking yellow invoice. It's got nothing to do with me. I can't relate to it. Sometimes I get all the way to Leicester Square before I turn round and go back again. I can't keep still on the tube. I can't take all those people staring out of the corner of their eye. It's no good looking at the paper. I can't cope with the news. There's no way I can take all those poor sods killing each other in Africa and Ireland and out in the Middle East. It's just as bad in the office. They're running each other down all the time. It's getting on top of me. I wish they'd give me the sack. They keep on offering me promotion. I haven't got the heart to turn it down. But I don't want it. I don't wanna know. I wanna be left alone. [*He sobs.*] I just want to be happy.

DR WILSON: I've written you a prescription for Valium.

GEORGE: Oh, no, thanks. I can't have any drugs. I've got three planets in the twelfth house. That's the house of self undoing. I'm already on forty cigarettes a day and fifteen cups of Nescafe.

DR WILSON: That might have something to do with the increase in pulse rate.

GEORGE: Will the Valium make my heart slow down a bit?

DR WILSON: Perhaps you could try it and let me know how you feel. I'll see you again in a few days, George.

SCENE EIGHT

The lounge. WALLY, JANET *and* SYLVIA *are sitting down.* TREVOR *is walking up and down.* KIERAN *comes out of the male dormitory with* CYRIL. KIERAN *sits down.* CYRIL *hovers about.* VICKY *comes in and pins a piece of paper on the notice board: a notice about a forthcoming social.*

WALLY: What's that all about, Vicky?

VICKY: We're going to have a social in three weeks' time.

WALLY: We're not, are we?

VICKY: Yes. I hope you're all going to help with the preparations.

WALLY: Yes, of course. You just say the word. Whatever you want me to do.

VICKY: I'll let you know.

[VICKY *smiles and goes off.*]

JANET: How can you have a social in here?

WALLY: Oh, they've had 'em in here before. They all come in off the other wards. The doctors come out and all and have a dance. They have a buffet and a load of lemonade punch. [*He looks to make sure* TREVOR *is out of earshot.*] They can't have nothing stronger, though, because of the alcernolics.

SYLVIA: I might be able to sneak a bottle of something in on the quiet.

KIERAN: If you do you can bring me in a Guinness. I'll give you the price of it.

WALLY: You can get me one and all.

KIERAN: We'll have a bit of a hooley out in the lavatory.

WALLY: Oh, look out, here comes trouble.

[DR WILSON *comes in and goes up to* SYLVIA.]

DR WILSON: Shall I see you now, Sylvia?

[SYLVIA *goes off with* DR WILSON. TREVOR *starts kicking the furniture.*]

SCENE NINE

The psychiatrist's office. DR WILSON *and* SYLVIA *are facing each other.* SYLVIA *takes a letter out of her handbag.*

SYLVIA: I've got something to show you. [*She plonks the letter down on his desk.*] Look at that. Three rooms, kitchen and bathroom. D'you know what that place is? It's a bleedin' tower block. And look at the postal district. S.W.11. I asked for S.W.1. They can't read. D'you know where this is?

DR WILSON: It's Battersea.

SYLVIA: You might call it Battersea but I happen to call it Clapham Junction. I know that place. I've seen it from the bus. You'd have to be blind to miss it. One dirty great rotten tower block after another, stretching for miles. And you know the sort of blocks they are, don't you? The ones on legs. Twenty-five storeys stacked up on four little legs. Well, sod that for a lark.

DR WILSON: They ask you to go along and view the flat on the 17th.

SYLVIA: Well, you needn't think I'm going. It'd be a waste of time and a waste of bleedin' money.

DR WILSON: I believe the flats are very nice inside.

SYLVIA: Oh, don't give me all that rubbish.

DR WILSON: Surely it would be an improvement on where you are now.

SYLVIA: If I wanted to live up in the air, I'd go and build myself a nest up in the treetops.

DR WILSON: I would advise you to at least go and look at the flat, Sylvia. If you saw it you might change your mind.

SYLVIA: No I won't. I'm not going. And I'm not staying where I am.

DR WILSON: I think it might be a good idea for you to have another long talk with the Social Worker.

SYLVIA: Why?

DR WILSON: Well . . . because I don't think your problems are psychological.

SYLVIA: Oh, I see. That's a new one, isn't it. Huh. I've been seeing psychiatrists and taking anti-depressants ever since I left my husband but you think there's never been anything wrong with me. I've just been passing the time of day. Well, for your information I've been told I'm an anxiety neurotic by somebody with more experience than you've got.

DR WILSON: We'd like you to think about going home, Sylvia, within the next two weeks.

SYLVIA: Oh would you. Well, I haven't got a home to go to. It's a concentration camp. I don't know why they didn't put up a barbed wire fence and have guards patrolling up and down the verandas.

DR WILSON: I'm sorry, Sylvia. I can't wave a magic wand.

87

SYLVIA: No, but somebody in this hospital could if you asked them to. All it needs is for one big nob to pick up the phone and speak to another big nob. But you don't think I'm worth the effort, do you? Just because I haven't got a husband you think you can sweep me under the carpet with all the rest of the bleedin' shit. Well, you can't. You're gonna have to put yourself out a bit more.

DR WILSON: Have you thought about making an effort for yourself, Sylvia?

SYLVIA: Oh yes. If I had the money I'd go straight up to Harley Street and see somebody who knows what they're talking about.

[*Long pause.* SYLVIA *gets up and rushes out.*]

SCENE TEN

The female dormitory. OLIVE *is lying on her bed, humming a tune and eating chocolates out of a dirty paper bag.* SYLVIA *comes in. She goes to her bed, gets in and pulls the sheets over her head.*

OLIVE: D'you want a chocolate?
[*Silence.*]
I say, d'you want a chocolate?

SYLVIA: No, I bleedin' well don't. Just you leave me alone and mind your own business.

OLIVE: I could see the way you was heading from the day you first came in. I shouldn't be surprised if your troubles were all coming to a head.

SYLVIA: Shut up.

OLIVE: I'm only saying what I know. And I know. You mark my words, young woman. I haven't been proved wrong yet.

SYLVIA: Shut up! Shut up! Shut up! Shut up! Shut up!

> [SYLVIA *picks up an orange and hurls it at* OLIVE.]

OLIVE: Oh, you vicious old cow. Lucky that didn't hit me or I'd have you up in court. You'll pay for it, though. All in good time. Every bad deed you do comes back on you. Not once, not twice, but threefold. There's no getting away from him. The Lord of Material Trouble. He'll come and strike you down. He'll be coming like a bolt out of the blue.

> [SYLVIA *starts to scream.*]

You'll go all the way down until you hit rock bottom and you'll stay there until you've learnt your lesson, which will very likely take you the rest of your natural. And if you haven't learnt it by the time you pass on, you'll . . .

> [VICKY *comes in and goes up to* SYLVIA.]

VICKY: What's the matter, Sylvia?

SYLVIA: There's nothing the matter. Nothing at all. I'm just an evil old cow and my problems are not psychological.

SCENE ELEVEN

The lounge. Night-time. TREVOR *is playing* 'My Blue Heaven'. KIERAN *gets up and pulls* JANET *up for a dance.* WALLY *goes up to them and says "Excuse me".* JANET *walks away and leaves* KIERAN *to dance with* WALLY. GEORGE *comes out of the male dormitory in a long striped nightshirt. His hair is wet and he is carrying an astrological chart. He sits down next to* JANET.

89

GEORGE: I've done your chart, Janet.

JANET: Oh. Thank you very much.

GEORGE: You're a Gemini.

JANET: Oh. I was hoping you'd say I was a Cancer. I don't much like the sound of what I've read about Gemini.

GEORGE: You're a double Gemini, Janet. You've got Gemini rising as well.

JANET: I suppose that means I've got two lots of split personalities.

GEORGE: No, it doesn't mean anything like that. As a matter of fact, I've got Gemini rising myself.

JANET: Rising where, though?

GEORGE: It's the sign rising over the horizon at your actual moment of birth.

JANET: Oh, I see.

[KIERAN *and* WALLY *come over and sit down.*]

WALLY: What's that, George?

GEORGE: It's Janet's natal chart.

WALLY: Oh, it's very nice, isn't it. Look at that, Kieran. Look what he's done.

KIERAN: What the devil is all that about?

JANET: It's all about me and what I'm like.

KIERAN: Is that a fact? I don't know what they'll think of next. Ah well. Time to be hitting the hay.

WALLY: Yeah. I can feel the old Mogadon creeping up on me. Goodnight, Janet. Goodnight, George.

TREVOR: Goodnight.

[TREVOR *gets up and goes off.*]

JANET: Goodnight.

GEORGE: Goodnight.

KIERAN: Don't forget to put out the cat and lock the back door.

JANET: Eh?

WALLY: He's only pulling your leg.

[WALLY *and* KIERAN *go off.*]

GEORGE: What was I saying, Janet?

JANET: You were telling me about the horizon.

GEORGE: Oh yes. Right. You've got what they call a bucket chart. See your Venus up here in Taurus? That's the handle of the bucket. Now, there's your first house. Gemini. That represents your self. Your ego or whatever you want to call it. You've got the Sun, Mercury, Saturn and Uranus all in your first house. That's quite a heavy combination. Especially as your Mercury is retrograde and Saturn and Uranus are in conjunction. What that means is that every time you feel the urge to move yourself forward you get the urge to hold yourself back at the same time. So you find it very hard to make up your mind.

JANET: Yes, that is true, I suppose. No. It's not true really. I can make up my mind. Unless it's something you have to think about seriously. It's no good rushing into things.

GEORGE: It's no good hanging about either. Anyway, you've got your Sun here in the last degree of Gemini within orb of conjunction of Jupiter there, which is two degrees into Cancer. That's a good one for making a lot of money. What do you do for a job?

JANET: I've been doing temporary typing for a few months now. Since I left my last job. I got fed up with it. I'm trying to get into the BBC. I think it'd be a lot more interesting. What do you do?

GEORGE: Not a lot, really. I'm supposed to be in charge of the accounts in Shipping and Forwarding. But I couldn't give a shit about any of it. I don't think I'll be there for much longer, though. I'm writing a book.

JANET: Oh, are you? What's it about?

GEORGE: I don't like talking about it, really. You know *The Lord of the Rings?* Well, it's along those sort of lines. But it's different. It's about these people who live on a star. Only they're not like human beings. I hope I can get it finished while I'm in here. Now, where did I get to? The Moon is in the fourth house in Virgo. And so is Neptune. But unfortunately the Sun and Jupiter are forming a square with Neptune, so you're likely to be easily deceived by other people.

JANET: I don't think there's much chance of that. I might not look it but I can be just as crafty as everybody else.

GEORGE: You're not, though. And not everybody else is crafty either. I'm not crafty.

JANET: You wouldn't be very likely to admit it, even if you were.

GEORGE: You just said you were crafty, though, didn't you?

JANET: I didn't. I said I could be crafty if I had to be. Just like everybody else.

GEORGE: You probably attract a lot of crafty people.

JANET: No I don't. You are funny.

GEORGE: No I'm not.

JANET: You are. I've never met anyone like you before.

GEORGE: There's a lot of people like me. I'm nobody special.

JANET: Yes, but you're funny.

GEORGE: So are you.

JANET: I'm not. Does it tell you anything about what's going to happen in the future?

GEORGE: Yes, I'm coming to that. Going back to last
July 1st though, it looks as if there was some
sort of unsettled phase in your working life.

JANET: That's right. There was. That's when I left
Scotland Yard.

GEORGE: Where?

JANET: That's the job I had with the Metropolitan
Police. The one I got fed up with.

GEORGE: Oh, I see. Well you should have had some
improvement in your career on the 29th of
September.

JANET: I couldn't have had, though. I was in here.

GEORGE: You shouldn't have come in here at that
time. On the 29th of September, Jupiter was
forming a trine with Mars. That won't
occur again until the 2nd of January. Now.
On the 10th of October you'll be hearing
some good news in connection with a
friend.

JANET: The 10th of October? That's next week,
isn't it? Oh good. Does it say anything
about my . . . my love life.

GEORGE: No. Have you got a boyfriend, Janet?

JANET: Not at the moment.

GEORGE: I can't see anything much happening in the
near future.

JANET: I didn't actually break it off with the last
man I was going out with. I said I'd phone
him up. I still might. He's not really right
for me, though. I never meet anyone who's
right. Have you got a girlfriend?

GEORGE: I haven't got time. I need to be on my own a
lot. And anyway, I wouldn't want to get too
involved with a woman while Saturn is
going through Virgo. I'll probably start
thinking about marriage sometime around
the spring of 1981.

JANET: Have I got any prospects of ever settling down?

GEORGE: Well you haven't got any planets in your seventh house. That's the house of marriage. But if you look to the ruler of the seventh house cusp which is, what, Jupiter, you have to see if it's got good aspects. Hmm. Jupiter square Neptune. You have to be careful about being deceived, Janet.

JANET: Oh God. I wish I hadn't let you do the chart now. It's really depressing.

GEORGE: There are a lot of good things as well, though. It's not as complicated as my chart. Actually, Janet, I was looking at your chart in comparison to mine. And your Venus is right on my Uranus.

JANET: What does that mean?

GEORGE: Well, it's supposed to be something quite exciting. It's not necessarily anything to do with . . . I mean, I don't think it's always . . . You can't ever guarantee . . . I mean, we're not actually compelled by the planets, it's our own . . .

[*The* NIGHT NURSE *comes in.*]

NIGHT NURSE: It's time you two were in bed.

JANET: I'm not tired.

NIGHT NURSE: No, I don't suppose you are. I can't think why he's never put you down for a sleeping pill. He doesn't have to come in here at night.

GEORGE: I can't go to bed until my hair's dry.

NIGHT NURSE: You shouldn't be washing your hair at this time of night. You'll catch a chill. I'll see if I can borrow a hairdryer off somebody for you.

GEORGE: No, no, don't. I mustn't use a hairdryer. It has to dry naturally because of the perm.

NIGHT NURSE: What, you've had a perm?

GEORGE: Yes.

JANET: A lot of men have perms these days.

NIGHT NURSE: Well, it's the first I've heard of it.

GEORGE: I hope you don't think I'm gay.

NIGHT NURSE: It makes no difference what I think.

GEORGE: I'm not, though.

NIGHT NURSE: I don't care what you are as long as you go to bed at night.

> [*She goes off.* GEORGE *runs his fingers through his hair.*]

GEORGE: It's too short at the sides, isn't it?

JANET: No, it's fine. It looks nice.

GEORGE: You don't have to say that.

JANET: No, it does look good, George, really.

GEORGE: I told him not to take too much off. Bastard. He promised he'd only trim it. You can never trust any of them. I'm not ever going back there again. I won't feel right until it's grown another inch. You've got nice hair, haven't you.

JANET: It's all right. I haven't done much with it since I've been in here.

GEORGE: You've got nice teeth as well.

JANET: Oh. So have you.

GEORGE: They're not too bad considering the amount of trouble I've had with them.

> [*They stare at each other.*]

You've got a lot of little freckles on your nose.

JANET: Haven't you got long eyelashes.

> [OLIVE *comes into the lounge.*]

OLIVE: Nurse! Nurse! Nurse!

> [*The* NIGHT NURSE *comes running in.*]

NIGHT NURSE: No need to shout your head off. What do you want?

OLIVE: You'd better come in and see to her quickly.

SCENE TWELVE

The female dormitory. SYLVIA *is sitting on her bed, cutting a tee shirt into pieces. There is a pile of clothes all over the place, also cut up into pieces. The* NIGHT NURSE *comes in.*

NIGHT NURSE: Now, what's all this nonsense? Oh, look at these lovely clothes all ruined. Give me those scissors.

[*She struggles with* SYLVIA *and gets the scissors off her.* SYLVIA *pulls everything off the bed and throws the mattress on the floor. The* NIGHT NURSE *struggles with her.* OLIVE *helps the* NIGHT NURSE *to restrain her.*]

SYLVIA: Don't you touch me! You old witch! Get her off me! Get her off!

[SYLVIA *kicks* OLIVE *and gets free. She runs out. The* NIGHT NURSE *and* OLIVE *run after her.*]

SCENE THIRTEEN

The lounge. JANET *and* GEORGE *are on the couch.* SYLVIA *runs out. The* NIGHT NURSE *and* OLIVE *run after her.* SYLVIA *starts smashing the place up.* GEORGE *gets up and helps the* NIGHT NURSE *and* OLIVE *to restrain* SYLVIA. *He gets hold of her, puts his arm around her and sits her down. She sobs. The* NIGHT NURSE, OLIVE *and* JANET *clear up the mess.* WALLY *comes out of the male dormitory. He is fully dressed.*

WALLY: Good morning.

OLIVE: Get back inside. It's the middle of the night.

WALLY: What are you all doing up?

NIGHT NURSE: It's all right, Wally. You just go back to bed now, dear.

OLIVE: Well, go on.

WALLY: Don't you tell me what to do, you old bag.

OLIVE: Don't you talk to me like that or you'll be sorry.

WALLY: Well, don't you fucking well tell me what to do. You're not a nurse.

OLIVE: You mind your language. You foul-mouthed little nobody.

NIGHT NURSE: That's enough of that now, thank you very much.

OLIVE: He wants to go and wash his mouth out with soap.

> [OLIVE *goes into the female dormitory.* WALLY *shakes his fist at the door and swears under his breath.*]

NIGHT NURSE: Come on now, Wally. Get into bed and I'll bring you in a nice cup of Horlicks.

SCENE FOURTEEN
The psychiatrist's office. JANET *and* DR WILSON *are facing each other.*

DR WILSON: How are you feeling today, Janet?

JANET: I'm all right, I suppose. Sylvia's not going to do any more dancing. Well, you can't blame her, really. But I don't fancy doing any of those boring old things in O.T. When have I got to go home?

DR WILSON: Do you feel ready to go home, Janet?

JANET: I don't know. No, not really. But I thought

you might have wanted me to go. Do you think you could tell me what's wrong with me? You know that Irishman, Kieran O'Toole? He told me he was a manic depressive. And Sylvia says she's an anxiety neurotic.

DR WILSON: I see. You'd like a label. Well, I'm afraid I haven't got a label to give you, Janet.

JANET: You must think there's something wrong if you're keeping me in here and sending poor old Sylvia out.

DR WILSON: I've been wondering if it might be a good idea to send you along to see the psychotherapist.

JANET: Oh.

DR WILSON: I can only recommend you for an interview. Whether or not you would benefit from treatment would have to be for the psychotherapist to decide.

JANET: What sort of treatment would it be?

DR WILSON: It would involve a number of sessions talking to the psychotherapist in much the same way as you talk to me but on a rather more intense level of discussion. I don't know how you feel about the idea. It can be quite a painful process.

JANET: Why do I have to have it?

DR WILSON: I'm not totally convinced that you do. Psychotherapy demands complete co-operation from the patient as well as a real desire for improvement. And there is a long waiting list, I'm afraid.

JANET: How long would the treatment take?

DR WILSON: Six months or so. It does tend to vary a great deal.

JANET: Why would it be painful, though?

DR WILSON: You might have to look at things in yourself that might be upsetting in order to find out and understand why you've been getting those funny feelings.

JANET: I haven't had any funny feelings at all since I've been in here.

DR WILSON: Are you sleeping under the sheets now?

JANET: No. But I can get under the bedspread. I'm scared in case they might come back. And I still think it must be something physical. I don't know how you can be so sure if you haven't given me any proper tests.

DR WILSON: I've treated a lot of people with all sorts of funny feelings. People get these symptoms when they're anxious and unhappy about their lives.

JANET: I'm not all that unhappy about my life. It's just ... Well, I know I'd be all right if I could find the right person.

DR WILSON: One wonders why the idea of marriage is so all-important.

JANET: It's not natural to stay single, is it? You're married.

DR WILSON: Yes, but ...

JANET: Yes and so are most of my friends. And some of them are not all that wonderful-looking either. It doesn't seem fair. I wanted to have some children. It's dangerous to have your first baby after the age of thirty, isn't it?

DR WILSON: I'm afraid the National Health Service can't give you a prescription for a member of the opposite sex.

JANET: Is that meant to be funny?

DR WILSON: Just a little joke. All I'm saying, Janet, is that I can't wave a magic wand.

JANET: I haven't asked you to. I didn't think you were a fairy.

[*Silence.*]

99

DR WILSON: ⎱ I'm afraid . . .
JANET: ⎰ I can't . . .

JANET: What did you say?

DR WILSON: You were going to say something.

JANET: It doesn't matter. You probably wouldn't have understood anyway. Whatever I try to say to you it comes out all wrong. We don't ever seem to get anywhere.

DR WILSON: No, we don't.

JANET: I don't know what you want me to say. No matter what I say to you you don't seem a bit sympathetic.

DR WILSON: Why should I be sympathetic? I think if you're so desperately keen to find a husband you should make a bigger effort to find one.

JANET: Oh yes? Where? Out of a computer? Or do you expect me to put an advertisement in the paper?

DR WILSON: Why not?

JANET: You must be joking. I've got a bit too much respect for myself to do a thing like that. You must know the sort of people who put those ads in the paper. They're freaks. They're people who come to London looking for something a bit kinky.

DR WILSON: They could be just lonely people, Janet. Like yourself.

JANET: I'm not lonely.

DR WILSON: I think you are. I think you're a very lonely and vulnerable young woman.

JANET: I am not. I don't know how you could say such a thing. You don't know anything about me. You don't know where I live and you don't know the sort of life I lead. I've got loads of friends. People are always asking me out. I've only got to pick up the

phone and I could be out with a man
tonight.

DR WILSON: Well, I suggest you do that, Janet. Go out
and have a jolly good time.

JANET: I will if I want to. And I wouldn't come back
in here again afterwards. I want to go home.
I want to be with my friends. I know you
think nobody cares about me but they do. A
lot of people think I'm all right. I'm going
home. I definitely am. I'm fed up with
being in here with a crowd of loonies. And
you're every bit as bad. You're the most
insulting man I've ever met.

[JANET *gets up and marches off.*]

SCENE FIFTEEN

The female dormitory. SYLVIA *is in her bed
with the sheets over her head.* OLIVE *is lying
on her bed.* JANET *comes in and starts to
pack her suitcase.*

OLIVE: Are you going, dear?

JANET: Yes, I am.

OLIVE: I thought you wouldn't last long.

[JANET *starts to throw things into
her case.*]

JANET: Where's my jar of wheatgerm? I left it on
here. I know I did. Who the hell's taken it?
You can't leave a bloody sodding thing in
here!

[VICKY *comes in.*]

VICKY: What's the matter, Janet?

JANET: I'm getting out of this looney bin now. I'm
not gonna be treated like an idiot. And I'm
not gonna be insulted by that bastard of a
Dr Wilson.

VICKY: Would you like to tell me what's upsetting you?

JANET: No, I wouldn't. You'd only be on his side. You're all as bad as each other. And I've lost my jar of wheatgerm. Somebody's taken it. They're all a load of thieving bastards in here.

VICKY: Let me help you to fold these things up properly.

JANET: No. I can do it by myself.

[CYRIL *comes in.*]

CYRIL: What's wrong?

JANET: I'm going home.

CYRIL: Why? What's happened?

JANET: Nothing. I just want to go.

VICKY: Shall I order a taxi for you, Janet?

JANET: No. I'm going on the tube.

CYRIL: Will you have a cup of tea before you go?

JANET: No, I won't.

CYRIL: Do you want a cup of tea, Vicky?

VICKY: Yes please.

[CYRIL *goes off.*]

VICKY: Sit down for a minute, Janet.

JANET: No.

VICKY: I think we'd all feel happier if you went in a calm state of mind instead of storming out in a temper.

JANET: You don't like me, do you?

VICKY: Do sit down for a minute.

JANET: No. I knew you didn't like me when I first came in. What is it you don't like about me?

VICKY: I'll have to tell Dr Wilson you're going. I expect he'll want to give you a prescription for some Valium.

[VICKY *goes off.*]

JANET: You bitch.

[OLIVE *comes over with a bag of chocolates.*]

OLIVE: You have one of these, dear. Go on. Tuck in. I'll have one with you. They've been upsetting you again, haven't they?

JANET: You should have heard the way that Dr Wilson spoke to me. He said I ought to advertise for a husband in the paper.

OLIVE: Well, he's a man, dear. Never discuss your romantic affairs with a man. You can always discuss them with me.

JANET: I don't think I can be bothered any more.

OLIVE: Yes you can. What about the chappie from Liverpool?

JANET: Who? Oh. The one from Birmingham, you mean.

OLIVE: Yes dear. You didn't light the candle like I told you to.

JANET: You can't light candles in here. They'd think you were trying to set fire to the place.

OLIVE: I'll tell you what you can do, dear. But you'll need an apple. And a large sheet of paper. You write down the letters of the alphabet then you put the piece of paper on the floor. You stand with your back to the paper, then you pick up the apple and you try to peel it all in one go. Then you shut your eyes and you throw the peel over your left shoulder. Whichever letter it lands on, that's the initial of the man who's intended to be your legal partner. It's never been known to fail, dear.

JANET: Have you ever done it for yourself?

OLIVE: Yes, dear. I tried it but the peel wouldn't land on any letter. It rolled right over on to the floor. I was fated to be single.

JANET: Oh blimey. I'd better not try it then.

OLIVE: You can always make do with second best and take a lover. You couldn't in my day or you were an outcast.

JANET: Have you got an apple?

OLIVE: No. But she's got some over there. Go on. She won't miss one.

[JANET *gets an apple off some-body's locker.*]

JANET: I haven't got a large sheet of paper.

OLIVE: Use that nice big carrier bag, dear. Start writing your letters out. I'll go and get you a knife.

[OLIVE *goes out.* JANET *writes the letters of the alphabet on a paper carrier bag.* CYRIL *comes in with a cup of tea.*]

CYRIL: Where's Vicky?

JANET: I don't know.

CYRIL: What are you doing, Janet?

JANET: I'm not doing anything.

CYRIL: Oh. You can have this cup of tea if you like.

JANET: Ta.

[CYRIL *goes to the door and meets* OLIVE *coming in with a knife in her hand.*]

CYRIL: What are you doing with that knife?

OLIVE: I'm going to cut your little dickie off.

[CYRIL *backs away.*]

OLIVE: Haha. That made you jump.

CYRIL: You give me that knife, now.

JANET: It's for me, Cyril. I'm going to peel an apple.

OLIVE: You go and get on with some nursing, dear. We want to be left alone.

CYRIL: If you're going to peel an apple, I'll watch you peeling it.

JANET: We can't very well do it with him standing there.

OLIVE: Oh, let him watch. He'll be none the wiser. Go on, now. Peel the apple, dear.

> [OLIVE *puts the carrier bag on the floor and* JANET *peels the apple and throws the peel over her left shoulder.*]

JANET: I daren't look. I bet it hasn't landed on a letter.

OLIVE: Oh yes it has. It's landed on the letter V. [*to* CYRIL] Here's your knife. Now go and spy on somebody else.

> [CYRIL *goes off.*]

JANET: There's not many names beginning with a V. Victor ... Vincent.

OLIVE: It could be somebody foreign, dear. They're the best.

JANET: How do I know for sure if I will ever meet him, though?

OLIVE: I can only tell you what I know, dear. And I know certain things. He's out there waiting for you somewhere. And I'll tell you something else. It's what I say to all the young brides. Add a drop of blood to his dinner of a Friday night. Your own blood, dear. Just the one drop. You do that and he'll never leave you.

JANET: I couldn't do that.

OLIVE: Yes you could.

JANET: Do I owe you any money?

OLIVE: No, dear. Unless you want to give a small donation.

JANET: Yes, of course. How much?

OLIVE: Whatever you like, dear ... 50p.

> [JANET *gives* OLIVE *fifty pence.*]
> Thank you very much, dear.

SCENE SIXTEEN

The lounge. MRS O'TOOLE *is sitting on the couch with her knitting.* WALLY *is sitting next to her.* KIERAN *is asleep in a chair.* TREVOR *is walking up and down with a bottle of milk.*

MRS O'TOOLE: Is there any sign of that one getting out of the bed?

WALLY: No. They don't seem to be taking no notice of her.

MRS O'TOOLE: Oh, they're wise to all them old tricks.

WALLY: She hasn't been having nothing to eat.

MRS O'TOOLE: I bet she's got something hidden away in the bedside locker.

WALLY: She must have. You can't go without food for three days. I know I couldn't.

[JANET *comes in.*]

MRS O'TOOLE: Hello, Janet. We were just wondering how poor Sylvia was getting on.

JANET: She only gets up to go to the loo. She hasn't had a wash for three days.

MRS O'TOOLE: Oh, the slut. What that one wants to do is to hang her hat up on the quare fellow now while he's still going spare or she'll lose her chance. Has he been coming in to see her?

JANET: No. He keeps ringing her up but she won't speak to him.

MRS O'TOOLE: What about the other one? The one she goes out gallivanting with.

JANET: I don't know. I think she usually rings him up. D'you know what? I've got a feeling she might have taken my jar of wheatgerm. It was on my locker in there and now it's gone.

WALLY: You couldn't live off of that stuff. Perhaps we ought to take her in a sandwich. I could quite fancy something to eat myself. Yeah. I could just eat a nice big plate of steak and kidney pudding.

JANET: Oh no, Wally, you're making me feel sick.

WALLY: She hardly never eats no meat, this one. She don't know what she's missing, does she.

MRS O'TOOLE: Well, I must say there's nothing I like better than a piece of best rump steak when I can afford it.

WALLY: Yeah. Specially when all the blood is running out all over the plate and on to your chips.

JANET: Ugh!

WALLY: D'you like black pudding, Mrs O'Toole?

MRS O'TOOLE: Oh, I do.

JANET: Stop it, Wally.

WALLY: How about a nice big dollop of shepherds pie.

JANET: Shut up. Oh. Look . . .

[DENNIS *comes walking in.*]

DENNIS: Hello.

WALLY: Hello, Dennis. How are you?

DENNIS: I'm not so bad. How are you?

WALLY: Well . . . You know. Not so bad, considering.

[DENNIS *sits down.*]

DENNIS: I was down in Out Patients so I thought I'd just pop in and see how you were.

MRS O'TOOLE: It's nice to see you again, Dennis. You're looking very well.

DENNIS: Oh, thanks. I don't feel all that marvellous, though, really.

MRS O'TOOLE: Are you working, Dennis?

DENNIS: Yes. I'm back at my old job.

WALLY: Oh, are you?

DENNIS: Yes. [*to* JANET] How are you?

JANET: I'm all right, thanks.

DENNIS: Oh good.

[*Long silence.* TREVOR *walks past.*]

DENNIS: Hello, Trevor.

TREVOR: Hello. Are you getting on all right?

DENNIS: Yes, thanks. What about you?

TREVOR: I'm fed up with this bleedin' place.

[TREVOR *walks off.*]

DENNIS: Has somebody got my bed?

WALLY: Yes. A young fellow. George. Friendly sort of bloke. He knows all about the whatsname. The stars. You know.

DENNIS: What, the film stars?

WALLY: No, no. The er . . .

JANET: Astrology.

DENNIS: Oh. Oh, I know what you mean.

[*Long silence.*]

Oh well.

WALLY: I'm glad you're getting on all right.

MRS O'TOOLE: You're looking a lot better than you were.

DENNIS: How's Kieran getting on?

MRS O'TOOLE: He's much the same really. I don't think there's a lot they can do for him. I haven't been too well myself as a matter of fact.

DENNIS: Oh, I'm sorry to hear that.

MRS O'TOOLE: I had to go and see the doctor. He's put me on Librium.

DENNIS: Oh, I know.

MRS O'TOOLE: I wouldn't want Kieran to find out in case he'd worry and make himself worse. But to tell you the truth, Dennis, the doctor has warned me I'm heading for a nervous breakdown.

DENNIS: Oh dear.

MRS O'TOOLE: Don't say anything to him now, Wally, will you?

WALLY: No, of course I won't.

[GEORGE *comes out of the male dormitory.*]

GEORGE: Who wants a cup of tea?

WALLY: Oh, yes please, George.

JANET: And me.

MRS O'TOOLE: That would be very nice, George, thank you. Would you like a cup of tea, Dennis?

DENNIS: Er . . . No. No, I won't, thanks all the same. I'd better be getting off now if I want to miss the rush hour.

MRS O'TOOLE: [*to* GEORGE] Dennis was here before you.

GEORGE: Oh. Hello.

DENNIS: I had your bed.

GEORGE: Oh. [*to* MRS O'TOOLE] Shall I make a cup of tea for Kieran?

MRS O'TOOLE: You might as well in case he wakes up.
[GEORGE *goes off.*]

DENNIS: I'll probably see you again. I can always pop in for a few minutes if I'm down in Out Patients.

WALLY: Yeah. Right. Nice to see you again, Dennis.

DENNIS: Ta ta, then.
[*The others say goodbye.* DENNIS *goes off.*]

MRS O'TOOLE: I wonder is he living on his own or what?

WALLY: We should have asked him really, shouldn't we?

MRS O'TOOLE: I didn't like to ask him in case he might have turned on the tap. He was always shedding the tears, poor man. No wonder the wife went off and left him. God forgive me. I shouldn't be talking like that. But I bet he was an awful old woman to have to live with. I wonder if he sees the daughter at all? He missed her an awful lot.

WALLY: I would have liked to have had a daughter.

JANET: I'd like to have a little boy. With blond hair.

MRS O'TOOLE: I would have liked one of each but I'll have to content myself with the cat. Benedict we call him. That's the name I would have given a child. After the saint. But we left it too late. We were engaged for a long time. I don't know for how many years. He didn't have a very good job. If he had any job at all. I wanted a decent place to live. I didn't want to be living in some old lodging house. It'd be nice to have somebody else at home now to keep me company, especially in the evenings. Of course, I do a bit of visiting but you can't be out late on your own walking the streets of London. Not like the way you would at home. A lot of people used to come and see us. Only Kieran would fall asleep in the middle of a conversation and they wouldn't feel at ease sitting there, listening to him snoring and grunting. Look at him. I wonder what did I ever see in him? He might have been a different man altogether if the mother hadn't ruined him. She ruined the lot of them. When she wasn't running round attending to their bodies she was down on her knees sending up a stream of prayers for their immortal souls. I never seen such a devotion to the Mother of God. She had our Blessed Lady's picture hanging on every wall and a statue standing up in every corner. I don't think it was devotion at all. It was a disease. Wait till I tell you. No, I'd better not. Ah, I might as well, only you mustn't ever mention it to Kieran. His second name is Mary.

WALLY: It's not, is it?

MRS O'TOOLE: Oh, it is. I have it down in black and white. She named every one of the nine boys after the Blessed Virgin. He wouldn't like anyone to know.

110

[GEORGE *comes in with the tea.*]

I wonder have you any good news about Gemini?

GEORGE: Well, at the moment, Mrs O'Toole, you've got Mars, Uranus, Venus, the Sun and Mercury all in your solar sixth house of health and employment.

MRS O'TOOLE: Does that mean me health is going to be good or bad?

GEORGE: It could go either way. Depending on your individual chart.

MRS O'TOOLE: What I'd like to know is, if he's a Capricorn why hasn't he made a lot of money the way they're supposed to?

GEORGE: He might have some difficult aspects. A lot of people have. Look at me. I've got the Sun and Venus in opposition to Neptune. Roy Jenkins has got the same thing in his chart.

WALLY: Who? D'you mean him? The whatsname?

GEORGE: Yes. He's had quite a few disappointments the same as I've had. We have to keep on climbing back up again.

WALLY: My mother's changed over to the Conservatives. Well, the last time they had a whatsname they come and picked her up in the car and took her down there. She never had that with the Labour Party.

[KIERAN *starts punching the air in his sleep.*]

MRS O'TOOLE: What are you doing. [*She shakes him.*] Who are you having a fight with?

KIERAN: What?

MRS O'TOOLE: You were having a good scrap with somebody.

WALLY: There's a cup of tea there for you, Kieran.

KIERAN: Oh, thanks. I was out in the Wild West with

111

Jane Russell. Did you ever have that kind of a dream, Wally?

WALLY: Oh yes. I once had a dream about being in bed with the woman behind the counter in the paper shop. I don't know why I should have picked on her. I mean, she's all right but ... you know. I couldn't go in there afterwards. Not without blushing. I haven't had any dreams since I come in here.

GEORGE: You're probably not remembering them, Wally. We have to have dreams every night. To sort out the problems of the day.

WALLY: I don't know what that one was supposed to have sorted out for me. It only made it embarrassing for me to go and get my *Daily Mirror*.

JANET: I have ever such a lot of dreams about being in a foreign country. Only you always have to get there by going up in a lift or walking through a door in the library. I've been to China up in a lift. And I've been to Greece and some of the Arab countries. But I've been to America the most times. It must be from watching so many Hollywood films.

KIERAN: I think we're two of a kind, you and me.

GEORGE: I have a lot of discussion dreams myself. Lots of people sitting around talking.

MRS O'TOOLE: Isn't that what you do in the daytime and all?

GEORGE: Yes. But I seem to have a more colourful mind during the day. My dreams are always a bit of a let-down.

MRS O'TOOLE: I wouldn't like to see inside that brain of yours. It must be whizzing round all the time picking up bits of things like a Hoover sucking in the dust.

GEORGE: I know. I wish I could turn it off.

WALLY: I had to get her a new Hoover last Easter. She's not happy with it, though. I said to her, I said, don't get one of them uprights. They don't get properly into the corners. She would have one, though. Now she says she wishes she'd got a long one again. She makes out it was me who talked her into the upright. It wasn't me, I swear to you it wasn't. It was him. That Irish geezer in the Electric Board giving her all the old flannel. Oh, no offence to yourself Mrs O'Toole.

KIERAN: I know them kind of Paddies. They make me feel ashamed.

MRS O'TOOLE: He must have been from County Cork.

KIERAN: I bet he was.

GEORGE: I think why my brain goes so fast is because I've got Mercury in the ninth house forming a semi-sextile with Pluto. Intellectual chaos. Luckily, though, I have got Mars and Neptune forming a grand trine of earth with Uranus. Although I could do without having Uranus in my twelfth house. That's where Adolf Hitler had his Uranus. I suppose I could have been a bit of a dictator. No I couldn't. I've only got one planet in my seventh house. Hitler had quite a few planets in his seventh house. So did Mussolini and Stalin. And several other dictators as well.

WALLY: Here, have we had a biscuit with this cup of tea, or haven't we? I don't remember having one.

JANET: No, you didn't. D'you want one?

WALLY: I'll have one if anybody else is having one.

JANET: Do you want a biscuit, Kieran?

MRS O'TOOLE: He doesn't. He has his tea drunk.

KIERAN: I will have a biscuit, Janet, thank you, dear.

And we'll have a dance tonight. She's a great little dancer.

JANET: Oh, you're a much better dancer than me.

KIERAN: Isn't it a wonderful idea not to be letting any visitors in to the social.

MRS O'TOOLE: You could ask her for a date if they'd let you out.

KIERAN: If I wanted to ask anybody for a date I would, and I wouldn't need to get your permission. Where would you like to go, Janet?

MRS O'TOOLE: Ah, stop it. Will you stop showing me up.

KIERAN: Showing up. Oh, be Jesus Christ in Heaven, you want blowing up.

MRS O'TOOLE: God forgive you. Stand up till I see if I need to start decreasing for the armholes.

KIERAN: Aaah!

> [KIERAN *stands up while* MRS O'TOOLE *measures her knitting.* TREVOR *walks past and kicks the furniture.*]

GEORGE: Of course, Hitler had a badly afflicted Venus. His Mars was afflicted too. So was his Saturn. At least I have got Saturn in conjunction with Jupiter. The same as Shakespeare.

WALLY: Oh, you've got something in common with Shakespeare, have you?

GEORGE: Yeah.

WALLY: I used to think he was a load of old rubbish. I couldn't make head nor tail of what it was meant to be about. It's funny that because I find it hard to follow a lot of what you come out with.

KIERAN: I was in a lot of his plays.

MRS O'TOOLE: When was that?

KIERAN: Back at home. I was in the *Midsummer*

Night's Dream. I took the part of Demetrius.

MRS O'TOOLE: I didn't know you had a theatrical past.

KIERAN: You don't have to be knowing everything, do you? And what would you understand about Shakespeare?

MRS O'TOOLE: I understand a lot more than you think. I sat and watched *Hamlet* on the television. And you were snoring away.

KIERAN: That's only because I'd seen it before. And I was in it.

MRS O'TOOLE: You were not.

GEORGE: A lot of astrologers think that Jesus must have had Saturn and Jupiter in conjunction.

WALLY: What, like you and Shakespeare?

GEORGE: Yes.

MRS O'TOOLE: Now that's going a bit too far. You mustn't be talking like that about Our Blessed Lord. Jesus was the Son of God and God wouldn't need to have a horoscope done for himself.

GEORGE: I don't believe he was God.

MRS O'TOOLE: Oh!

[*She makes the sign of the cross.*]

GEORGE: I'm sorry, Mrs O'Toole, but I'm not a Christian.

MRS O'TOOLE: Oh. You'll have to forgive me, George. I didn't realise you were Jewish. You don't look it. Why didn't anybody tell me?

GEORGE: No, I'm not Jewish, Mrs O'Toole. I'm not anything specific. But I probably am a Buddhist by nature.

JANET: I quite like the idea of being a Buddhist.

GEORGE: You know you've got a retrograde Mercury, Janet. What that means in a karmic sense is you've got some negative mercurial traits carried over from some of your past lives.

JANET: Oh, I wonder who I was in the past?

MRS O'TOOLE: I don't like to hear that kind of talk.

KIERAN: They have a right to believe what they want to believe.

WALLY: I don't believe in Jesus Christ, neither. I don't believe in none of all that. I reckon when you die that's it. Kaput.

MRS O'TOOLE: Well, of course not everybody is given the gift of faith. I couldn't have got through my life without it. If I was given the opportunity I'd lay down my life for my religion.

KIERAN: You would not.

MRS O'TOOLE: I would and so would you.

KIERAN: Don't be telling me what I'd do. If Jesus came down again tomorrow, they'd bring him in here.

GEORGE: People with Jupiter and Saturn in conjunction in the twelfth house usually find themselves in prisons and mental institutions. It's a special kind of suffering we have to go through.

KIERAN: We must all have the same thing, then, if we're in here.

GEORGE: No, we haven't actually. Janet's got Saturn in her first house. In conjunction with Uranus.

JANET: And his Uranus is on my Venus, isn't it?

GEORGE: Yes it is. But I meant to tell you, Janet, that my Sun squares your Ascendant.

JANET: Oh.

KIERAN: 'So should the murder'd look; and so should I, Pierc'd through the heart with your stern cruelty: yet you the murderer look as bright, as clear as yonder Venus in

her glimmering sphere.' That's what I had
to say.

MRS O'TOOLE: It's a pity it didn't get you very far.

JANET: You said it very nicely.

WALLY: Fancy calling a little boy Mary.

KIERAN: What did you say, Wally?

WALLY: Oh, nothing.

MRS O'TOOLE: He's talking to himself. Did you know,
Wally, that the Jews have to have all the
blood drained out of their meat?

WALLY: Oh yes. They have special butchers and all,
don't they? Have you ever had a salt beef
sandwich, Mrs O'Toole?

MRS O'TOOLE: I have not. And I don't intend to have one
either. There's a Jewish man down at the
bottom of the road and he has two wives.

KIERAN: He has not at all. One of them is the
cleaning woman.

MRS O'TOOLE: That's what you think. They each have a
son and both them boys are the spitting
image of him.

KIERAN: Don't be talking through your hat.

MRS O'TOOLE: I know what goes on in that house. You can
see right in through the window when
you're walking past.

WALLY: Oh, look out. Here comes trouble again.
[DR WILSON *comes in and goes over
to* KIERAN.]

DR WILSON: Shall I see you now, Kieran?
[KIERAN *goes off with* DR WILSON.
MRS O'TOOLE *gets a bottle of pills
out of her handbag.*]

MRS O'TOOLE: This is what I have to take. Librium. [*She
swallows a pill.*] Have you seen him yet,
Janet, running around without a stitch?

JANET: No, I haven't.

MRS O'TOOLE: I bet he looks an awful sight.

117

SCENE SEVENTEEN
The psychiatrist's office. KIERAN *and* DR
WILSON *are facing each other.*

KIERAN: I think if ever a man missed his way in life,
it was myself. I don't know why I didn't go
on the stage when I had me chance. That's
all I'm fit for, Doctor. Standing up and telling a joke and giving them a bit of a ballad.
I threw me opportunity away. I always
thought I would do it one day. I can hardly
believe I didn't and now I'll never be able to.
I'm getting old and wizened and I'm going
mad in the head. Everybody thinks I'm
mad. I can see from the way they look at me
whenever I go back there and into the pub.
They know I'm only out for the weekend
and they're waiting to see will I start
attacking them or throw a fit and smash up
all the glasses. I'd like to go and live somewhere else. I should never have left home in
the first place or maybe I should have gone
away to America. What I'd really like more
than anything else in the world now is a
divorce. But I wouldn't get one, would I?
Not with a brother a priest and a wife
studying to be a saint. I wonder would I get
a separation on medical grounds?

DR WILSON: Would you like to have a word with the
Roman Catholic chaplain?

KIERAN: I would not. I've nothing to say to them
fellows. Unless I could persuade him to
speak to the wife and tell her to stop coming
in here and pestering me every day of the
week. But I bet he wouldn't. Oh, I must
have been the biggest fool not realising

118

what I was letting myself in for. D'you
know what I imagined, Doctor? I thought if
we ever had a fight it'd be the way Maureen
O'Hara loses her temper with the two eyes
flashing and we'd end up having a bit of a
wrestle. I never imagined I'd have to listen
to a voice nagging on about the walls and
the woodwork and the floors and the hole in
the roof. She sends me to sleep. But I'm not
allowed to sleep when I want to. Not when
I'm in me own house. Why the devil do I
have to go to bed and get up at the same time
as her? You wouldn't think we were a
husband and wife. You'd think we were a
pair of Siamese twins. Are you happily
married yourself, Doctor?

DR WILSON: Er . . . yes. Yes, I am.

KIERAN: You're a lucky man, so you are. Oh, I don't
know what I'm going to do.

SCENE EIGHTEEN
The female dormitory. JANET *is getting
dressed for the social.* SYLVIA *is lying on her
bed.*

JANET: Aren't you going to come out then, Sylvia?

SYLVIA: No. I might. No. Bugger it.

JANET: I shouldn't think it's gonna be all that
exciting.

SYLVIA: I couldn't come out anyway. I haven't left
myself anything to wear.

JANET: You can borrow anything you like of mine
if there's any chance at all it might fit you.
I'm not bothering too much. I don't want to
look as if I'm making a big effort.

SYLVIA: There's nobody out there to make an effort

for. Apart from George. I quite like the look of him.

JANET: Do you? He's all right, I suppose. I think he fancies me. But I'm not really bothered. I wouldn't want to start anything up with a person out of here. I know I'm in here myself, but . . .

SYLVIA: He'd be no worse than anyone outside. If you're not interested, I wouldn't mind . . . No. I can't go out there.

JANET: He keeps saying things to me. Like . . . Well . . . like he said his Venus was on my . . . or was it my Venus? I don't know. But one of our Venuses is supposed to be on the other one's Uranus, whatever that means. I think it's just his way of . . . you know. He could be telling you anything, really. I don't think he knows as much about astrology as he likes to make out. He told me I'd be getting some good news on the 10th of October. Well, I waited all day and nothing happened. Huh. I'm gonna send away for a horoscope. I know it's a lot of money. Thirteen pounds. But at least you do know you're getting a proper one. If George was any good, he'd be charging money. He is quite good-looking, I suppose. But he's not the sort of person I could really get involved with. And anyway, I've got a very strong feeling that I'm gonna be meeting somebody special quite soon. I reckon it's worth waiting for the right person. Have you definitely broken up with Brian?

SYLVIA: No. Not really. I would if something better turned up. He'd die if he heard me say that, poor sod.

SCENE NINETEEN

*The lounge. Just outside the lounge the
social is in progress. Disco music is being
played and people are chattering.* GEORGE
*comes into the lounge with a glass of
lemonade punch and a sandwich. He is
wearing a paper hat.* JANET *comes into the
lounge from the female dormitory.* TREVOR
is walking up and down.

GEORGE: Hello.

JANET: Hello.

[*Pause.*]

Have you been dancing?

GEORGE: No. Have you?

JANET: No.

GEORGE: I thought you would be.

JANET: No. There's too many funny looking
people out there. I did go out there but they
all started staring at me.

GEORGE: Oh.

JANET: I wouldn't mind having a dance if there was
anyone to dance with.

GEORGE: Well . . . I'm not much good at . . .

JANET: I wasn't asking you to dance.

GEORGE: I didn't say you were.

JANET: Well, I wasn't.

GEORGE: I must go and get another sandwich. D'you
want one?

JANET: No thanks.

[GEORGE *moves off.* VICKY *comes
in.*]

VICKY: George, come and have a dance with me.

[GEORGE *goes off with* VICKY. *The*
NIGHT NURSE *comes in wearing her
uniform with a paper hat.*]

NIGHT NURSE: [*to* JANET] All on your own? Here. Put this on. [*She puts a paper hat on* JANET.] Look a bit more cheerful. You ought to be dancing. Go and have a dance with Trevor. Come on now, Trevor. You go and have a dance with Janet.

> [*The* NIGHT NURSE *pushes* JANET *and* TREVOR *out of the lounge.* WALLY *comes in with a pile of sandwiches. He sits down.* DR WILSON *comes into the lounge.*]

DR WILSON: Hello, Wally.

WALLY: Hello, Doctor. Would you like a drink?

DR WILSON: Oh yes. Why not.

> [KIERAN *comes in.* WALLY *goes off.*]

Hello, Kieran.

KIERAN: Hello, Doctor.

DR WILSON: Having a good time?

KIERAN: Oh yes, thanks.

> [JANET *and* TREVOR *come back into the lounge.*]

DR WILSON: Hello, Trevor.

TREVOR: Hello.

DR WILSON: Hello, Janet.

JANET: Hello.

> [WALLY *comes in with a drink for* DR WILSON *and a paper hat.*]

DR WILSON: Thanks, Wally. Cheers.

WALLY: Good health. Would you like one of these, Doctor?

> [WALLY *gives the paper hat to* DR WILSON, *who puts it on and smiles at everyone amiably. There is rather a long pause.*]

DR WILSON: [*to* WALLY] Have you heard the one about the two psychiatrists? One says to the other: "I hear they're bringing in a case of catatonic schizophrenia today." "Oh, thank God," says the other one, "I'm getting sick of all this lager."

[*They all laugh.* GEORGE *comes in.*]

WALLY: A man goes to see a psychiatrist. He's got bananas behind his ears, cucumber slices up his nose and half a pineapple balancing on his head. He sits down calmly and says: "I've come to see you about my brother."

[*They all laugh.*]

DR WILSON: They're holding a schizophrenics' conference in Brighton next week but I'm in two minds about going.

[*They all laugh except* WALLY.]

WALLY: Why's that? Oh.

[WALLY *laughs.*]

KIERAN: Mrs Murphy goes to see the doctor about her stomach that was playing her up. "Oh that's nothing at all," says the doctor. "It's only a little bit of old flatulence. You'll be right as rain in no time at all." Nine months later Mrs Murphy was out wheeling a pram when she saw the doctor coming along the street. "How are you getting on, Mrs Murphy?" says the doctor. "Oh, I'm fine thanks," says Mrs Murphy. "What's that you've got in the pram?" says the doctor. "Oh, that's nothing at all," says Mrs Murphy. "It's only a couple of farts with bonnets on them."

[*They all laugh.*]

TREVOR: Doctor, doctor, I'm a pair of curtains. Pull yourself together.

[*They all laugh.*]

WALLY: A nutcase goes into a looney bin with a jelly, a sponge and a custard balancing on his head. The psychiatrist looks at him and says: "I say, my good man, do you realise that perched upon your head there is a jelly, a custard and and a sponge?" "Oh, don't mind me," says the nutcase. "I'm a trifle mad."

[*They all laugh.*]

DR WILSON: One psychiatrist was showing another psychiatrist round his hospital. They go into a work hall where a patient is dangling from the ceiling. His feet are on the plaster, his head is hanging down. "Good heavens, who's that?" asks the visiting psychiatrist. "Oh, don't worry," says the other one. "He thinks he's a light bulb."

[WALLY *laughs.*]

Er . . . "Well, why don't you let him down?" asks the visiting psychiatrist. "What!" says the other one. "And let us all work in the dark?"

[*They all laugh, less spontaneously than before. Then follows a long silence.* OLIVE *comes into the lounge and goes up to* DR WILSON.]

OLIVE: Could I have the next dance, Doctor?

DR WILSON: Oh, certainly.

[DR WILSON *goes off with* OLIVE. TREVOR *gets up and starts walking up and down.*]

WALLY: He's not so bad really, is he?

KIERAN: He's all right.

[KIERAN *looks round furtively then brings out half a bottle of whisky from his jacket. The bottle is half empty.*]

KIERAN: D'you want some of this, Wally?

WALLY: Oooh, have you drunk all that by yourself?

KIERAN: Sssh.

WALLY: Well, I couldn't take it neat. You'd better pour a drop in the gnat's piss.

> [KIERAN *pours some whisky into* WALLY's *glass.* GEORGE *goes over to* JANET.]

GEORGE: Do you want another drink, Janet?

JANET: No, I don't, thank you.

GEORGE: I had to have a dance with Vicky.

JANET: Yes, I saw you.

GEORGE: I bet I looked silly, didn't I?

JANET: I don't know. I wasn't taking any notice.

GEORGE: If you still want to dance . . .

JANET: I don't.

GEORGE: Well, nor do I.

> [JANET *moves away.* OLIVE *comes in with* DR WILSON, *who waves to everyone.*]

DR WILSON: Goodnight.

> [DR WILSON *goes off. They all call goodnight to him.* OLIVE *sits down next to* WALLY.]

OLIVE: There's a lot of perverts out there.

WALLY: Is that right?

OLIVE: I can spot a pervert a mile off. Have you locked up all your belongings?

WALLY: Oh yes, I definitely have.

OLIVE: They go to the toilet and help themselves to anything they see lying about. I've got all my valuables on me.

> [OLIVE *opens her cardigan to reveal her entire collection of jewellery.* CYRIL *and* VICKY *come in.*]

VICKY: Goodnight.

CYRIL: Goodnight. Have a good time.

> [CYRIL *and* VICKY *go off. The* NIGHT NURSE *comes in.*]

NIGHT NURSE: That's right. You go home and leave it all to the night staff as usual.

> [*The* NIGHT NURSE *bustles about clearing away empty cups and plates.* KIERAN *sits down.* JANET *goes over and sits next to him.*]

KIERAN: Hello there. Where have you been?

JANET: Nowhere.

KIERAN: You're looking very smart tonight.

JANET: Oh. Thanks.

KIERAN: I've never seen you looking so nice.

> [KIERAN *smiles affectionately at* JANET *then bursts into song.*]

'My young love said to me my mother won't mind
And my father won't slight you for your lack of kind
As she stepped away from me, oh this she did say
It will not be long, love, till our wedding day.
Last night she came to me, my dead love came in . . .'

> [KIERAN *breaks down and sobs.*]

JANET: Don't cry, Kieran.

> [JANET *breaks down and sobs with* KIERAN. *Outside the lounge people begin to sing the hokey-kokey, while* KIERAN *and* JANET *are continuing to weep.* WALLY *offers a sandwich to* KIERAN. TREVOR *walks up and down and kicks the furniture as the hokey-kokey goes on. The lights go down gradually.*]

THE END